HIDDEN
CAPE TOWN

HIDDEN
CAPE TOWN

PAUL DUNCAN
ALAIN PROUST

Published in 2013 by Struik Lifestyle
(an imprint of Random House Struik (Pty) Ltd)
Company Reg. No 1966/003153/07
Wembley Square, Solan Road, Cape Town, 8001, South Africa
PO Box 1144, Cape Town, 8000, South Africa

www.randomstruik.co.za

Reprinted in 2014

ISBN 978 1 43170 299 2 (Print)
ISBN: 978 1 43230 279 5 (ePub)
ISBN: 978 1 43230 280 1 (PDF)

Publisher: Linda de Villiers
Managing editor: Cecilia Barfield
Design manager: Beverley Dodd
Designer: Helen Henn
Editor: Gill Gordon
Proofreader: Bronwen Leak

Reproduction: Hirt & Carter Cape (Pty) Ltd
Printing and binding: 1010 Printing International Ltd, China

ACKNOWLEDGEMENTS

The author would like to thank the following for their help in making this book possible: Abubakr Shabudien, Discover Islam Centre, Cape Town; Alf Rhoodie, Lodge de Goede Hoop; Anita Shaw, Centre for the Book; Basil Bey, Bishop's Diocesan College; Captain Francois Morkel, Castle of Good Hope; Captain John Dorrington, Cape Town Rifles (Dukes); Captain John Manning, Cape Town Rifles (Dukes); Celeste Vorster, NGK Tafelberg; Christopher Peter, Director, Irma Stern Museum; Cynthia Court, City Hall; David Hart, Environmental Resource Management Department, City of Cape Town; Deon van Zyl, GK Hof Street; Mandla Matyumza, Centre for the Book; Dr Petre Prins, Prins & Prins Diamonds; Esther Esmyol, Iziko Museums of Cape Town; Ethne Julius, New Somerset Hospital; Fr Nikolai, Greek Orthodox Cathedral; Franklin James, St George's Cathedral; Hayden Proud, Iziko Museums of Cape Town; Hayley Bond, Amazing Spaces; Ingrid Pakendorf, Evangelical Lutheran Church; Pier and Jo-Marie Rabe; Linda Ruhle, Evangelical Lutheran Church; Lisa Dyason, Lisa Dyason Communications; Louise Ings; Lucy Campbell; Melody Kleinsmith, Iziko Museums of Cape Town; Major Stephen Brimacombe MMM, Cape Town Rifles (Dukes); Mary van Blommenstein, Curator: UCT Works of Art Collection and UCT Irma Stern Museum; Nikki Heath; Penny Murdock, Prins & Prins; Revd Dr Pieter Bingle, Gereformeerde Kerkgebou, Hof Street; Solly Burger; Tanya Barben, Curator, Rare Books and Special Collections, UCT; Wieke van Delen, Iziko Museums of Cape Town; Yasmine Jacobs.

Front cover: NGK Tafelberg; pages 2–3: NGK Tafelberg; page 5: Irma Stern Museum; back cover: Old Mutual Building.

CONTENTS

INTRODUCTION

This is a book about Cape Town's interiors. It's about all kinds of places, from public buildings to centres of learning, places of worship to museums, that perhaps it never occurred to you to pop into, even just for a quiet moment. Spanning the centuries from the 17th to the 20th, the range is enormous. This is the book you don't have.

Cape Town has a rich architectural heritage. Have you ever stopped for a moment and wondered what lies beyond the façades of the buildings you most probably drive past every day? Our city, like any other, is often just the wallpaper in our lives, and yet there's artistic, political, social, cultural, commercial and scientific life going on in those places; sometimes in extraordinary interiors. They might be characterized by a magisterial dome, a set of frescoes, a period look, a carved staircase, a collection of furniture, or a set of tiles. *Hidden Cape Town* is about these places, many of them the unsung heroes providing the backdrop to public life.

I've tried to stick to the city's centre, although that's been quite hard when the occasional outpost in one of the old suburbs was too tempting to exclude. Groote Schuur is one, Welgelegen another. There's probably another book anyway. *Hidden Cape Town Part 2* could easily be filled with buildings peppering the route to Simon's Town. There's also easily a book on Cape Town's many churches. I've cherry-picked places to feature from a long list of contenders, trying to highlight excellence over the commonplace, or the unusual over those of which there may be many other examples. Others I've disregarded, not because I'm a philistine, but because their intrinsic value is debatable or their interiors have nothing to contribute, either because they've changed irretrievably or because they've gone.

The title, *Hidden Cape Town*, could imply that the places you see featured are intentionally hidden from view. In most cases, as I discovered, this simply isn't the case. Many are not inaccessible either; it's just that as everybody rushes past getting on with life, there isn't much thought for what lies beyond a familiar entrance. I suppose this is inevitable, given that central Cape Town is only now coming back to life after decades as a place to avoid. What has survived is often nothing short of miraculous if you think about what has already been lost and what we have nearly lost.

Some places are well known and celebrated because they're great buildings with magnificent interiors. One is the Evangelical Lutheran Church in Strand Street, where Anton Anreith's massive statues of Hercules hold up a pulpit. While these sculptures are a reason to visit, so is the fact that its interior is virtually untouched by the passage of time and new discoveries are constantly being made in its archives. Another wonderful building is the former Metropolitan Methodist Church in Greenmarket Square. Now called the Central Methodist Mission, it's regarded as a masterpiece of Gothic Revival architecture both inside and out. And there's the Old Mutual Building, which, although difficult to get into, is regarded internationally as an iconic piece of Art Deco.

Others are popularly visited for their celebrated contents. The museum in Koopman's-de Wet House is one, the Old Town House, housing the Michaelis Collection of Old Master Dutch and Flemish paintings is another. Go and see Frans Hals's *Portrait of a Woman:* could this be one of the most significant paintings in Cape Town? But what about the portrait of Theodorus Bas Jacobi, also in the Michaelis Collection? Only recently it was confirmed as being the work of Jacob Adriaensz Backer – one of Rembrandt's more illustrious competitors and a sought-after and highly fashionable artist in his own day.

OPPOSITE: Sculptor Anton Anreith's work can be found in a number of Cape Town's historic buildings, including the Lodge de Goede Hoop, where his *Bereavement*, depicting a widow mourning the loss of her son, survived a fire in 1892.

After 400 years in obscurity, this painter has re-emerged from the shadows and this portrait, whose authorship has long been shrouded in mystery, is now something to celebrate. Are there other treasures lurking in this magnificent collection of Old Master paintings that costs only R10 to visit?

There are places that are less well known, other than to those who use them. The Lodge de Goede Hoop is one, Herbert Baker's Welgelegen is another. Here hang James Durdan's paintings; the only record of what Baker's interiors looked like when the Currey family lived there. And then there's the 18th-century Huguenot House in Loop Street, now the home of Prins & Prins Diamonds. Its past was painstakingly unravelled as layers of old paint were peeled away to reveal the remains of a previously magnificent range of decorated interiors.

There's the Nederlandse Gereformeerde Kerk Tafelberg in Buitenkant Street which, whenever you drive past, is locked and silent though clearly not abandoned because it's kept in good condition. Curiously, it doesn't even look like a church. Get inside – permission is given if you go to the office that you can only get to via the multi-storey carpark next door – and the massive hall-church with its hammer beam roof takes your breath away. Maybe I've just been blind all these years, but I never knew it was there. A series of small associated rooms are still painted in shades of Victorian brown with furnishings to match. Another of Cape Town's secrets is the interior of the Gereformeerde Kerk Hof Street, a work from the 1950s by that seminal Afrikaans architect Gerard Moerdyk. Utterly pure in its simple modernity, its gently curving lines are a poetic rendition of a liturgical formula that needed expression through a centrally focused auditorium. Nothing inside it is out of place. It's as beautiful now as the day it was completed. Hidden amongst the trees alongside the Mount Nelson's gates, it stands detached, silent and unobtrusive.

There are the curiosities. One of them, the Palm Tree Mosque in Long Street, has been there for nearly 200 years, but few people other than the faithful have ever been inside it. Not that it's anything special architecturally speaking, but the fact that it's still there – the most remarkable survival in the centre of the city – is something to celebrate. More so because its essential use hasn't changed in all that time either. In fact, it's busier than ever. The Castle of Good Hope is also full of surprises. One of them, the Cape Town Rifles (Dukes) Officers' Mess, continues a military presence in the old fortress of Cape Town, and it houses a museum containing the memorabilia of what is, in fact, the Cape's oldest infantry regiment. In the museum, Edward Rowarth's magnificent portrait of Colonel Cecil James Sibbett, the regiment's first Honorary Colonel (1935–1967) and at one period Private Secretary to Cecil John Rhodes, is magnificent.

Another curiosity lurks inside the New Somerset Hospital. There, the Lady Loch children's ward contains a gallery of paintings donated in 1900 by benevolent citizens who, in their Sunday art circles, painted scenes from familiar nursery rhymes and fairy tales for the entertainment of the beleaguered little patients. A hanging committee was appointed to arrange them on the walls where they remain to this day. If the children weren't transfixed by the characters from Sing a Song o' Sixpence – the king in his counting house, the queen in her parlour or the maid in the garden hanging out the clothes – they could watch through their ward's Tudor-style windows the rough Atlantic breaking on the African shores not far away. Today, the Lady Loch Ward is empty; who knows what these delightful paintings' future holds?

And then there are the interiors – amongst them some magnificent ones belonging to the University of Cape Town – not included because budgets wouldn't cover the enormous fees required in return for permission to photograph. I'm thinking of Smuts Hall, its dining hall and common room in particular. The Houses of Parliament aren't here either, although not for want of trying. There was a mountain of red tape, and then there were those emails that went backwards and forwards and back again, asking me to resend already sent documentation over and again, getting me nowhere in a byzantine show of pointless inefficiency, only to be told that my request to photograph had been declined. What a pointless waste of everybody's time; those individuals in the secretary to Parliament's office should be ashamed of themselves. The interiors of the Parliament building are magnificent and deserve an airing in a book such as this one. Another interior that didn't make it into the book is that of the old General Post Office in Darling Street. Those enormous painted panels by Sidney Carter and GW Pilkington were left out because we couldn't find a way amongst all the market clutter around them to photograph them effectively.

Inevitably there are more churches than there are mosques or synagogues and, while some interiors achieve a keyhole view of a moment in history (Bertram House is one) others, like the Centre for the Book, are alive again after a lifetime in mothballs and are full of renewed purpose. Still others are just waiting for a new lease of life: surely it's time to do something about the City Hall, one of the last great civic town halls thrown up by the British Empire? It desperately needs something new to do. I've walked through those vast halls. I've seen the panelled mayor's chamber, in which hangs Terence McCaw's lovely portrait of Mayor Bloomberg's wife, along with Neville Lewis's *Malay Man*. I've seen the coloured marbles, the jeweled tesserae on the floors and the ornate white stucco, and I've gained a sense of the pride that went into its construction at the turn of the last century. I've even watched an elderly man from Wiltshire, stripped to his tie and braces, a specialist in tower bell music, play the 39-bell carillon housed in the clock tower. Operated by an antiquated array of wooden levers and pedals that require enormous skill to play, it's been silent for so long that only a much older generation of Capetonians will ever have heard it. It's the last working carillon in South Africa. A restored city hall, reinvigorated and put to good use, will bring this unique instrument – and this part of Cape Town – back to life.

Something that astonishes is just how prolific Herbert Baker was. His buildings may be more prominent elsewhere, but here in Cape Town, apart from one or two obvious exceptions, they're almost reticent. And there are lots of them, although I've chosen to feature only Groote Schuur, Welgelegen, St George's Cathedral, UCT's Hiddingh Campus – where there's a glut of them, and bits of Bishops (Diocesan College). What else is clear, however, is that there are also one or two unsung architectural heroes in Cape Town. Charles Freeman, who designed the Metropolitan Methodist Church, is one, and James Morris, architect of the South African Reserve Bank, now the Taj Hotel Cape Town, is another. Dig a little deeper and both these men were responsible for more than just a little of what central Cape Town looks like today.

A real surprise for me was the interior of the Old Mutual – that dark and somewhat forbidding ziggurat in Darling Street. Now mostly apartments, nonetheless the miles of labyrinthine corridors and endless circuitous staircases didn't prepare me for what lay behind the chained and padlocked aluminium doors on the eighth floor: a room, not big, but double-height, its walls adorned with towering frescoes depicting Cape Town's history in gorgeous autumn colours, its floor the perfect parquet. As the golden early morning light streams in through those characteristic perpendicular, projecting triangular windows, the reason why *Hidden Cape Town* had to exist received the best affirmation there could be. Going into that assembly room for the first time suddenly made this book seem worthwhile. There, hidden from view, embalmed in the gloom of a now defunct office building, the subject matter of its decoration not the most politically correct, is one of Cape Town's greatest treasures.

PAGES 8–9: Many of the interior furnishings at Groote Schuur survive, along with period fittings and embellishments, but perhaps the time has come to dispense with later intrusions – like the wall-to-wall carpet.

PAGES 12–13: At the Greek Orthodox Cathedral, a collection of antique and mid-20th-century paintings and icons adorns the screen separating the sanctuary from the nave. At the centre of the upper register, a depiction of the Last Supper is flanked by the Twelve Apostles.

Ο ΑΓΙΟΣ ΦΑΝΟΥΡΙΟΣ
Η ΑΓΙΑ ΑΝΝΑ

GROOTE KERK
Adderley Street

Is it Gothic or is it neoclassical? From the outside, the mother of all Dutch Reformed churches in South Africa is the oddest mixture. Even its plan has its own peculiarities: what began as a Greek cross is now a rectangle – you can still see bits of the former entangled in the construction of the latter. Originally that Greek cross plan had gables at the end of each arm. Today only the clock tower survives from that period.

When the church was built (the foundations were laid in 1678), the Dutch Reformed Church monopolized religious practice at the Cape. The small size of the settlement, and its Calvinistic preference for unadorned settings and simplicity of worship, meant that there was little incentive to construct many or large places for worship so, as late as 1795, there were still only five churches in the whole place. The Groote Kerk was built essentially as a 'preaching box': the idea was that as many worshipers as possible, seated in their box pews, would have a good view of a centrally located, elevated pulpit constructed with sounding boards that will have helped in the preacher's being heard. The design of these pulpits often inspired the creation of elaborate structures; the pulpit in the Groote Kerk is a really good example of one. Here raised on a pedestal of lions it's a triumph of the work of Anton Anreith (1789), a sculptor who began life in the Dutch East India Company's employ as a labourer and who ended up renowned for his accomplished high-baroque style of work. Another sculpture, also by Anreith, has survived inside the Lutheran Church in Strand Street. In these preaching boxes, galleries at the back or along the sides were sometimes added in an effort to bring more of the congregation closer to the preacher. Internal ornament was sparse, owing both to theological inclination and a lack of abler artists.

The influence of this building lasted well into the 19th century, partly because the religious sentiments and cultural tastes of the white settlers were conservative. In 1779 it was enlarged: the re-entrant walls were removed and large, circular columns were placed at the old corners. In the 1830s it was rebuilt again, acquiring its rectangular form. Dedicated in 1841, it remains today substantially as left by Hermann Schutte (*c.*1761–1844), its latest architect and builder.

OPPOSITE: The stairs lead to the galleries, one on either side of the gigantic interior space above the main doors, and added as the congregation expanded. Originally, the less-elevated sat up here, the box pews below were the domain of those of high rank who could afford to pay for them.

PAGES 16–17: At funerals of leading citizens, hatchments – on which were emblazoned the coat-of-arms of the deceased – preceded the funeral procession. After burial, they were hung inside the church and vestry. Only 25 original hatchments survive, beautiful heraldic mementoes so oddly out of place in Africa.

NATVS est
D= 20= November
1684
OBIIT D= 5
Februarÿ
1751

FREDERICK RHENIVS, CAPATAIN MILITAIR,
NAT 9 1. 2 IAN. 1694
OBIIT d. 4 DEC
1754

PAGES 18–19: The vast interior houses Anton Anreith's handsome Burmese teak pulpit. When the original church was demolished in about 1838, the pulpit was encased in a wooden box and left where it was while demolition, and then construction, carried on around it. Hermann Schutte's plaster ceiling defies gravity; dome-like, it covers an area of 1 023m^2 unsupported. The organ is modern.

LEFT: The site of the church was formerly a cemetery and, in later years, the dead filled the crypts. Indeed, Simon van der Stel himself is buried here (d.1712), as is Ryk Tulbagh (d.1771). This magnificent tombstone belongs to another Dutch governor, Pieter Baron van Reede van Oudtshoorn (d.1773).

THIS PAGE: Hanging on the wall to the right of the pulpit, *The Last Supper*, by Dutch painter Lambert Jacobsz (1598–1636), was discovered hidden in the clock tower.
PAGE 22: The box pews are accessed by a little door with a latch. In the past, those sitting there kept the chill at bay using hot coals brought into church by their slaves. The riempie chairs survive from the original church.
PAGE 23: Modern stained glass lights up the interior today, but the design and colour copy the 19th-century stained glass still in the windows of the vestry facing onto Bureau Street.

BESPREEK
49

MOUNT NELSON HOTEL

Orange Street, Gardens

The Mount Nelson Hotel occupies what's left of an 18th-century estate that once straddled the mountain end of Government Avenue. Its owner for a chunk of the 19th century was one of the wealthiest men at the Cape, Hamilton Ross, who owned two prominent Cape Town properties – this one, and Sans Souci in Claremont. The Mediterranean-pink hotel today has his old homestead at its nucleus.

Ross had arrived from England in 1796 and, by 1798, had scandalized the locals by eloping to Madras with the daughter of a venerable VOC official. The event was noted by Lady Anne Barnard in one of her letters to Henry Dundas, secretary of war, in which Ross, in spite of his behaviour, is described as 'a young man of very good character'. The couple married and returned to the Cape in 1803, where Ross became a successful merchant and, subsequently, a prominent citizen. Hamilton Ross bought Mount Nelson in 1843 for his daughter Maria Johanna and her family. There's a watercolour of its house and garden, painted by Maria, who received lessons from no less than Thomas Bowler, in the entrance hall of the museum at Bertram House – just across the road from the hotel's main entrance. When Maria's first husband died leaving her with four young children, she married her cousin, John Ross. Their eighth child, Ellen, born on the Mount Nelson estate, was the mother of Anne Lidderdale, the benefactress of the Bertram House Museum, who died in 1979 at the age of 99 and whose bequest to Bertram House also contains a portrait of Hamilton Ross.

The Mount Nelson's history of magnificent grounds, including a deer park, is faintly bucolic and was vividly recalled by Lidderdale, who spent many happy hours playing there as a child. Could anything be more appropriate, given that the hotel's gardens today are a lovely oasis of green in an increasingly built-up city?

Today, the Mount Nelson, a destination hotel that has survived from the colonial era, still has a faintly Edwardian air about it. It was bought in 1890 by shipping magnate, Sir Donald Currie, for use as a hotel by the First Class passengers on his Union Castle shipping line – the first ever South African hotel to offer hot and cold running water. Herbert Baker supervised its construction. However, within months of opening, in 1899, the Boer War started, and the hotel became the headquarters for the British Army. Lord Kitchener was based here, as were generals Buller and Roberts. During that time, the hotel was 'booked solid with senior officers, distinguished war correspondents, wives, sweethearts and even ordinary adventurers and sightseers', wrote James Sherwood and Ivan Fallon in *Orient-Express: A Personal Journey*. A young Winston Churchill was nursed back to health here by his mother, Jennie, after his escape from a Boer prison camp, and he filed a number of his dispatches from what he described as 'this most excellent and well-appointed establishment which maybe thoroughly appreciated after a sea voyage'. Other familiar names in its guest book are those of Rudyard Kipling, Arthur Conan Doyle, HG Wells and Cecil John Rhodes. In 1956, it became part of the Cayzer empire, and in 1988, Orient-Express Hotels bought it.

The hotel was decorated in much the same way for decades, until about six years ago when it was decided it needed a shake up. 'The trick was not to throw the baby out with the bathwater – aesthetically speaking, that is,' says the man charged with its redecoration, Graham Viney. 'A cocktail lounge, the Planet Bar, was installed and at the same time the adjacent lounge lost its mustard and pink colour scheme that had survived since just after the war. The fitted carpets were lifted, wooden floors relaid and the panelling was painted in eight shades of white to lighten and brighten the enclosed east-facing room.'

OPPOSITE: The vaulted Garden Room is the hotel's original dining room. Today, it is used for formal lunches, gala dinners, presentations and performances. At the far end is a portrait of Queen Alexandra.

LEFT: A grand piano tinkles away in the background, decorator Graham Viney's white-on-white lounge the effervescent setting to an old-world ritual: high tea. Colonial gentlemen and denim-clad rock stars, genteel ladies and barely dressed young wives all head for the profiteroles and the chocolate torte.

PAGE 28: The hotel gardens evoke distant memories of the former park-like surroundings of Hamilton Ross's country house which, in their heyday, were populated by deer and incorporated a number of fountains.

PAGE 29: The elegant Planet Bar is a popular cocktail lounge overlooking the terrace and gardens.

NEDERLANDSE GEREFORMEERDE KERK TAFELBERG

Buitenkant Street

Is it a church? Is it a house? From the pavement on Buitenkant Street, this extraordinary building looks like one of those overwrought, high-Victorian mansions you see at the heart of somewhere like Graaff-Reinet, built when cash was flush and taste was a scarce commodity. In fact, it is an NGK church, built in 1892 to a design by the architect HT Jones who, in the process, seems to have mixed most of his design metaphors. The exterior hides a most unexpected interior.

Its richly pedimented façade is simply a massive screen hiding an enormous, high-roofed hall running at right angles to the street. You enter up a short, wide flight of steps that stretches between two high bay windows topped by neoclassical pediments buttressed by florid Flemish scrolls, into a narrow ceramic-tiled foyer that leads to the main hall. More ecclesiastical-looking within than without, its interior comes as a complete surprise. Driving past, you're simply not aware that it exists at all; could it be one of the unsung treasures of this city? A high cast-iron gallery that's reached by a wooden spiral stair overlooks the massive hall, its roof supported by timber king post hammer beams and trusses with trefoil motifs. High windows lining the hall filter the light through simple, colour-blocked stained glass – notable if only because they're a singular note of colour in an interior that's brown, brown and brown again.

NGK Tafelberg is a huge hall-like church that began life as a mission hall, the Cornelia *Zaal*. Along with the adjoining Cornelia House (for needy women), the William Frederik School (which closed in 1907), and an apartment along the front on the second floor, it was given in trust to the Nieuwe Kerk by Susanna Maria Hertzog in memory of her parents, William Frederik Hertzog and Susanna Cornelia Hertzog (born Hiddingh), with the stipulation that when a self-supporting congregation came into being in the area, it would be transferred to them. Dr JJ Kotzé, Dr Andrew Murray and Professor Marais conducted the inauguration ceremony on 27 January 1893. Miss Hertzog had the privilege of unlocking the door. Although services were held here regularly, the Tafelberg Congregation was only founded in 1944, 47 years after the death of Miss Hertzog, and it is thriving today. A footnote to the history of NGK Tafelberg is this: the Revd. JD (Koot) Vorster, brother of the former Prime Minister and State President, Advocate John Vorster, was the congregation's minister from 1935 until his death in 1982.

OPPOSITE: The organ has always been a feature of the NGK Tafelberg. It was installed in 1892, and has 1164 pipes and a walnut case. The innards have subsequently been renewed.

RIGHT: A complex, ornate high-Victorian cake of a place, NGK Tafelberg is more homestead than church. Way larger than life, the great bay windows house both Cornelia House and the William Frederik School.

THIS PAGE: A spiral wooden staircase in perfect condition leads up to the gallery.
OPPOSITE: The entrance foyer, where the faithful congregate before entering the church, is paved with ceramic tiles incorporating biblical references, amongst them symbols of the Agony, the Crucifixion and Judas's Betrayal of Jesus.

LEFT: The church interior: in reality, just a high hall whose roof is supported by timber king post hammer beams and trusses.

OPPOSITE: The gallery is supported by cast-iron pillars and there's a cast-iron balustrade along its front. The original furniture, which is still *in situ*, came from Boston in the United States of America.
THIS PAGE: The vestry on the Commercial Street side of the church is just one of a range of associated buildings that are still in use, among them a school and meeting rooms.

FOUNDER'S HOUSE, BISHOPS
Rondebosch

Founder's House is the oldest part of Bishops. It's at the core of the Diocesan College, founded by Bishop Robert Gray in 1850 and soon referred to as the Bishop's school. A school for boys, it began life informally in 1849 at the bishop's own house, Protea (now known as Bishopscourt), up on Wynberg Hill. But tiring of little boys continually under foot, Gray opened two new schools: one for white children at Woodlands, a pine-studded Rondebosch farm where Bishops now is (and where many of the old pines have survived), and one for black children, on the site of today's Zonnebloem College above the city bowl. The purpose of the new school at Rondebosch, the Collegiate School of the Diocese of Cape Town, was 'to give a sound education to the Youth of the Colony', and it would be conducted strictly on the principles of the English Church. It would take boys only, 'not under 10 and not above 15 years of age.' The Bishop's wife, Sophie Gray, recorded that when the school opened it had six pupils. It didn't really prosper until Canon George Ogilvie, from St George's Grammar School, which was attached to Cape Town's St George's Cathedral, arrived to become headmaster in 1861.

The focus of Founder's House is the Quad. Walking through it on a winter's day you could be at an English public school or an Oxford college. There's a monastic look about the place which, I suppose, isn't a coincidence, given that this is a Church school. With only three sides originally, the Quad remained the school's focus until Canon Ogilvie enlarged it in 1863, adding a new classroom on the south side of what is now called the Mount Nelson and, on the north side, a kitchen and a dining hall with a dormitory overhead. In the mid-1890s, the fourth side was completed. In 1896, Herbert Baker completed the first section of the roughly hewn stone façade, in 1905 adding a clock tower, over today's main entrance.

Canon Ogilvie is a Bishops legend: he fashioned what Bishops would later become. He also 'introduced rugby football to Bishops in 1861, and to South Africa as well,' says Basil Bey, former housemaster at School House, rugby coaching legend and today a curator of the Bishops museum. 'Bishops was first with it – although many other schools will say that they were. In those days we played the Winchester version of rugby football which was more of a kicking game – quite a brutal game in fact – while our opponents, the military team from the garrison at Wynberg Camp, played the Rugby version. In the end we swapped over, a move Ogilvie wasn't happy about.' In the early years, the game was played on the Rondebosch Common. Rugby thrived, if only because the Bishops teams needed others to play against. The local press, however, had no great hopes for the new Rugby Union in South Africa, for in the Cape Town *Daily News* of July 18th, 1876, it was reported that 'the new game will hardly prove a very popular one at the Cape ...'.

Oh well, if you were a dud at rugby you could always have looked after some of the animals kept in the school's menagerie. Anthony Trollope, visiting in 1877, found at this 'school in Rondebusch ... a perfect menagerie of interesting animals attached ... which is an advantage which English schools seldom possess.'

OPPOSITE: The dining hall (1862), one of the oldest sections of the Founder's Quadrangle, was panelled in 1957.

ABOVE: A master's study at Founder's House. The bolt hole of a memorabilia-collecting magpie, it has a steep Gothicky roof and small upper-floor windows. Rugby balls commemorate a sport nurtured in its infancy in South Africa by Bishops' players.
OPPOSITE: The Brooke Wing of the Founder's Quadrangle – in a style known cheekily as Collegiate Gothic. A cloister was planned for the Quad side of it. It houses the former chemistry laboratory, designed by Herbert Baker (1896).

LEFT: The main entrance to the Quadrangle is through a gate in the Brooke Wing, designed by Baker & Massey (1904). Above the arch is the clock tower.

SO SÊ
DE
HERE

SENDINGGESTIG MUSEUM
Long Street

This is one of the loveliest buildings in Cape Town. And to think it was very nearly demolished to make way for a car park. Your heart stops when you hear what they wanted to do – and often did – in the 1970s. One of the oldest churches in South Africa that still exists in its original form, it was nearly lost when the hotel next door needed room to expand. By then, its congregation had largely been resettled on the Cape Flats – in fact, it was proposed that a replica be built in a coloured township on the fringe of the city. We're lucky that it is still standing.

The Suid-Afrikaanse Sendinggestig was built in 1804 by the South African Missionary Society, an offshoot of the Dutch Reformed Church. Its primary purpose was to convert slaves to Christianity by providing religious and literacy instruction, and this was the first official slave church in the country. For over two centuries, slaves formed an integral part of daily life at the Cape. They were builders, artisans, coopers, food vendors, fishermen, grave diggers, water carriers, wood collectors, gardeners and porters. Even modest homes would have owned a slave or two, perhaps a housemaid, or a nursemaid for the children. It is estimated that 63 000 slaves were imported between the mid-17th century and the early 19th century.

The building's magnificent façade, designed by FW de Wet, with its fluted Corinthian pilasters, dentilled cornice, plaster swags and urns, is one of the high points of Cape Town's city centre. Although it is much smaller, it bears a strong resemblance to the façade of Strand Street's Lutheran Church, both of which are essentially large halls for preaching in. Along with the Groote Kerk, these venues all had a similar liturgical purpose in that they were 'preaching boxes' dominated by a pulpit, in this case, a wonderful neoclassical one approached by a double flight of steps.

Fortunately, the Sendinggestig, or Old Slave Church – now one of the oldest surviving buildings in Long Street – was saved from the fate of much of old Cape Town, given national monument status and turned into the South African Mission Museum. Today, this gracious building plays an important role in commemorating the city's slave heritage. Nearby, you will find the Slave Lodge; a plaque in Spin Street marking the site of the Slave Tree, where slaves were auctioned; the Town House, from where important notices and proclamations concerning slaves were read; Greenmarket Square, where fresh produce was sold and where there was a fountain from which the slaves fetched drinking water; Platteklip Stream on Table Mountain, where they went to do the household laundry; and, on the corner of Darling and Buitenkant streets, the site of the Whipping Post, where slaves were tied while receiving corporal punishment. It is not always easy to reconcile the brutal reality of our past with the architectural treasures it produced.

OPPOSITE: The interior is dominated at one end by a pulpit (1824) and a gallery, made of yellowwood and stinkwood, that runs around the back and the two long sides.
PAGE 48: The façade on Long Street, a baroque edifice of great beauty, has a temple front articulated by four Corinthian pilasters on high bases.
PAGE 49: Saved from demolition in the 1970s, this delicate little church is no longer in use other than as a museum. The floor is made of slate quarried on Robben Island.

A.D.
1799

NATIONAL LIBRARY OF SOUTH AFRICA
Queen Victoria Street

George Basevi's Fitzwilliam Museum in Cambridge was the model for the design of what is today known as the National Library of South Africa, one of the most important buildings to have been erected in Cape Town in the middle of the 19th century. Greek Revival in style, its Corinthian portico preceded by a shallow flight of stairs, the building was designed by William Kohler (born *c.*1815) and opened in 1860, at a ceremony conducted by Prince Alfred, Queen Victoria's favourite son, whose portrait still dominates the main Reading Room.

A public library had originally been established by Government proclamation in 1818. It was managed by a committee that was empowered to raise funds by imposing a tax on every cask of wine passing through the Cape Town market. This tax was removed in 1828, and the library existed thanks to the largesse of local subscribers until 1862, when a government grant was made available.

Inside, it's hardly changed to this day. Take the computers, the posters and the bad office furniture out of the Reading Room and you have the establishment to which, in 1861, Sir George Grey, 'one the Cape's most urbane and enlightened governors', says Desiree Picton-Seymour, donated his private collection of about 5 000 books and manuscripts – thus forming the core of the new South African Public Library. There are medieval and Renaissance manuscripts and the collection contains, among other items, several humanistic manuscripts whose textual content is rare or unique. Caesar, Livy and Lucan, Boethius and Gregory the Great, Dante and Petrarch are all represented here, as well as several Books of Hours in Latin, French and Dutch. The earliest manuscript is a Latin Bible dating from the ninth century (*c.*875–900).

In addition to the Grey Collection, the National Library houses extraordinary collections of books, manuscripts, maps, photographs and works of art. The Africana Collection, in particular, is rich in older publications and includes records of the earliest sightings of the Cape by European voyagers, a collection of 18th- and 19th-century accounts of inland exploration (by, for example, Burchell, Le Vaillant, Livingstone, Sparrman and Thunberg), and books describing fauna and flora, dating from the 17th century to the present. The WHI Bleek Collection is, significantly, the first formal, in-depth study of any of the Southern African San languages. The library also houses maps and atlases, and books on every topic from shipping to slavery.

The wing to the right of the entrance portico was completed first. The one on the left, when it was finished, housed the South African Museum, which contained an eclectic array of just about everything you can think of, from birds' eggs and Ancient Egyptian relics to an embroidered Greek jacket once worn by Lord Byron.

OPPOSITE: Portrait of HRH Prince Alfred, Queen Victoria's favourite son, presented to the library on its opening in 1861 and signed by the artist, Frederick Say (b.1804). During his working life (1830–1860), Say was a fairly prominent society portrait painter, counting the Royal Family as his most high profile clients. After his death, in 1868, he seems to have been largely forgotten. This was one of his last major commissions; painted in commemoration of Alfred's visit to the Colony to inaugurate new harbour works in Table Bay.

RIGHT: The main Reading Room, dominated by Say's portrait of HRH Prince Alfred. Its companion piece is a large portrait of Queen Victoria, now in the Houses of Parliament. Kohler, the architect, was described by contemporaries as 'a draughtsman of great task' and, while working in the Colonial Engineer's Department, won the design for what would become the Public Library in an open competition.

LEFT: The National Library of South Africa houses extraordinary collections of books, manuscripts, maps, photographs and works of art.

OPPOSITE: A portrait of Sir George Grey in uniform, by Charles Gow, *c.*1861. The library was constructed at the instigation of Grey, whose collection of books and manuscripts formed the nucleus of its contents – becoming known as the Grey Collection: 'Being left to some new country, might prove to it a treasure of Great Value, to some extent helping to form the mind of each of its generations, as they come following on,' wrote Grey.

SIR GEORGE GREY

GEREFORMEERDE KERKGEBOU HOF STREET

Gardens

It's April 6th, 1952. The Gereformeerde Kerkgebou Hof Street is opening its new doors for the first time. Gerard Moerdyk is the architect. 'Presies 300 jaar gelede,' says the foreword in the event programme, 'het onder God se beskikking Jan van Riebeeck die ware gereformeerde leer, soos vervat in the heilige Skrif en die Drie Formuliere van Enigheid, geplant hier aan die suidpunt van donker Afrika. Die ware, suiwere, gereformeerde godsdiens het in beoefening gekom hier waar woestheid, afgodery en heidense barbaredom geheers het.' To mark this event, a cutout metal ornament of a ship, the *Drommedaris*, was fixed to the weather vane on the steeple to show the direction of the wind. The original *Drommedaris* brought Jan van Riebeeck, and thus the reformed teachings, to the Cape precisely 300 years earlier, on April 6th, 1652.

Who better, then, to express the role of the liturgy in the Reformed Church than architect Gerard Moerdyk (1890–1958)? Even today, he remains one of the best-known Afrikaans architects, but Hof Street is probably the least known of his churches. Moerdyk is known for two things: designing the Voortrekker Monument, near Pretoria; and designing a series of churches whose plan breaks with the usual cruciform arrangement, to seat the congregation around the pulpit, as it does here at Hof Street. He looked to the Byzantine period for inspiration, finding that the centralized plan of the eastern Orthodox Christian tradition best suited the purposes of Dutch Calvinism – where the liturgy centres on the preaching of the doctrine and the sermon, and so didn't require an apse for the sacramental ritual as in, say, the Roman Catholic Church. At Hof Street, the plan is effectively an amphitheatre whose focus, being the pulpit, emphasizes the preaching of the Word. And what makes it the perfect auditorium are the acoustics, the effectiveness of which in most of his ecclesiastical projects made Moerdyk something of a star.

Throughout his career, Moerdyk designed over 80 churches and, in his time, he was the unofficial 'official' architect of the Dutch Reformed Church. His distinctive style was hugely influential then and, while his work has often been copied, seldom has it been bettered. Today the Hof Street church still serves the community for which it was intended.

OPPOSITE: The creed of the congregation requires a plain, unadorned interior in which to worship. Unwittingly, perhaps, this enhances the beautiful simplicity of the architectural forms.

RIGHT: Moerdyk's work is characterized by its mixing of historical elements, which might be Byzantine inspired, neoclassical or even Gothic. Here you can see the influence of, say, something like the old Roman Baths of Caracalla. The large semi-circles supporting the roof and housing the windows give a sense of monumentality to what is in fact a very small building. The interior is an amphitheatre in which the seating focuses on the pulpit.
PAGE 60: The pulpit from above. It projects into the space so that the congregation has an unimpeded view of the preacher in it.
PAGE 61: The view from the gallery. The seating meticulously follows the outline of the architecture.

MOEDERSKAMER

DIE BYBEL
THE BIBLE

CITY HALL
Darling Street

The 1909 *Cape of Good Hope Official Handbook*, by town clerk Finch, describes the City Hall in Cape Town as being in the Italian Renaissance style. Hans Fransen, in his *Guide to the Old Buildings of Cape Town*, sees a French Renaissance influence. It may owe more to Leeds Town Hall (*c*.1854), in the UK, but a connection with something as pre-eminent as the Italian or even the French Renaissance is not to be sneezed at, a decent provenance being essential even in the colonies. It was thought originally that such an ornament to the city would be a fitting tribute to Queen Victoria in the year of her Golden Jubilee, 1887. Massive, dominated by an enormous clock tower, the City Hall is also a fitting symbol of an empire at its pinnacle. Cape Town was one of the last colonial cities to acquire a civic hall and it came into being full of the majesty of empire – the last major Victorian building to be erected in the city.

Occupying an entire city block, its setting is extraordinary. The conceptual juxtaposition of the unique site, set dramatically against a backdrop of Table Mountain and fronting onto the historic Grand Parade, with the nearby Castle of Good Hope reinforcing its strategic importance, 'was inspirational', writes former Cape Town Mayor, David Bloomberg. Essentially it replaced the little (by comparison) baroque-style Town House on Greenmarket Square about which everything was wrong for busy civic offices, and it is the result of a competition, held by the Cape Town Municipality in 1894, to which there were 17 entries. The winning scheme was by Harry Reid and Frederick Green, although the original design appears to have been very different from what was finally built. The Grand Hall, for instance, was then entered through the front of the building, which was also only two floors high. However, the new building was slow in going up: difficulties of the site, as well as the Anglo-Boer War, seem to have held up its construction until 1905. During these delays it seems that the present design materialised.

The richness of this building only really becomes apparent once you're inside – particularly the Grand Hall with its elaborately decorated ceiling and overwrought stuccoed wall surfaces. There were no compromises: marble columns, magisterial marble staircases, teak woodwork, well-proportioned offices, a dignified council chamber, with a press and public gallery, 'inspired pride in the citizenry and a building was born that in every way identified itself as Cape Town's City Hall,' continues Bloomberg. As a result, the city's epicentre moved from Greenmarket Square to the Grand Parade. The Grand Hall became the premier venue for family, civic and national celebrations, concerts, balls, religious services, eisteddfods, political meetings, protests and sporting events. In 1947, the Grand Hall was decorated in preparation for the visit by the British Royal Family – an event that inspired the redecoration of the Mayor's Parlour in a Cape Dutch style. Here too, the Cape Philharmonic Orchestra continues to play, over the years having attracted, amongst others, conductors and musicians such as Sir Thomas Beecham, Igor Stravinsky, Sir Charles Groves, Claudio Arrau and Yehudi Menuhin.

In its planning, it seems that the city fathers were unwise in providing insufficient space for a burgeoning municipal bureaucracy, and the lack of office space led to a post-war plan to demolish the City Hall and replace it with a bland, modernist box. Ultimately, the bland modernist box was duly constructed on the foreshore and the City Council decamped there. The City Hall was vacated by all but the orchestra. Today it fulfills a variety of peremptory functions and it has been all but mothballed. While the exterior was restored some time ago, its interior is still awaiting a new lease of life.

PAGE 62: The central 'winged' staircase – as the 'Programme of Inauguration of City Hall Buildings, 1905' described the stately ceremonial stair – leads from the Darling Street entrance to the municipal offices on first floor. Handsome balustrading, Sicilian marble for the treads, the dado capped in 'rouge royal marble', it is a 'noble staircase', continued the programme, for the benefit of ticket-holders admitted to the opening ceremony in the Grand Hall. *RIGHT:* The Grand Hall, 130 feet long, 61 feet wide and 55 feet high, was designed with a view to holding 'musical festivals, meetings of citizens, banquets, balls etc,' said the programme. The hall contains seating for 2 000 people and is encircled by a promenade corridor with four swing doors on each side.

PAGE 66: The building's corridors are lined with teak panelling, and the floors are of mosaic. *PAGE 67:* The Mayor's Parlour, on the first floor, received a makeover in time to welcome King George VI, Queen Elizabeth, and the princesses Elizabeth and Margaret, in 1947. Panelled in stinkwood and yellowwood, a jarring note today is the bizarrely patterned carpet. Antique Delft china and locally made antique Woodstock glass fill the shelves. The bronze bust is of former mayor Abe Bloomberg (1945–1947). *OPPOSITE:* King Edward VII and Queen Alexandra, committed forever to stained glass. *RIGHT:* A portrait of Mrs Bloomberg, by society portrait painter Terence McCaw, one of the unsung heroes of South African art.

ABOVE: In the Mayor's Parlour, controversy surrounds the origins of the Louis XV clock seen above the fireplace. Is it the one purchased in 1805 for the Council Chamber in the Old Town House, the one that went missing for about 60 years only to have been found in 1887 lurking in a forgotten cupboard, and then moved in 1905 to the new City Hall? Who knows?
OPPOSITE: The fireplace in the Council Chamber, a design hybrid if ever there was one, features a bit of Cape Dutch, some Arts and Crafts and a smattering of neoclassical.

ABOVE: At one time, the clock in the turret that soars way above the rooftop struck the hours and chimed the Westminster quarters. The time is shown on four iron dials 'filled with best opal'.
OPPOSITE: The former Council Chamber is now given over to a variety of different uses as the authorities make up their minds about the building's future.

PALM TREE MOSQUE

Long Street

At heart, 185 Long Street is an 18th-century house. It's rather an odd sight: incongruously domestic-looking in a sea of shops and nightclubs, a tall, lone palm at its door. The most striking thing about it is that it's there at all.

A lone survivor of a time when Long Street was lined with one- and two-storey houses, nothing much appears to have changed here over the last 250 years or so. Even the 18th-century sash windows still gaze out over the street, although the lower ones are just a few centimetres above the now-raised pavement level, and you have to descend into the building through a front door also adapted to the new height. Once, a low wall divided its little front garden from the road, and here stood the two palm trees that gave it its name. Just one survives.

Built as a house, it became a mosque early in the 19th century. 'The most extraordinary thing about the Palm Tree Mosque is the continuity it represents with the past,' says Abubakr Shabodien of Cape Town's Discover Islam Centre. 'Not only has its physical appearance changed very, very little over the years, but also the way it's used now is virtually the same as when it became a place of worship when two freed slaves, Frans van Bengalen and Jan van Boukies, who bought it in 1807, converted just one room into a prayer room. Today the upper floor is one large, undivided space, possibly an addition from around 1811, when more space was needed for a mosque.'

In all the old views of Long Street, there it is, a mosque without a minaret. Why no minaret? It dates from a time in Cape Town when Islam wasn't yet apparent in the appearance of its buildings, because religious practice, while not exactly concealed, wasn't entirely encouraged either. And, anyway, the building was still a private house. Even the Auwal Mosque in the Bokaap, the city's oldest, that began life in 1798 as a madressa, only much later acquired its minaret, Tuan Guru having called the faithful to prayer through an open window with a voice so loud and clear that, it was said, he could be heard in Simon's Town! Who needed a minaret?

'Since 1811, the house at no. 185 Long Street has been both home and place of worship. Even today, when it's time to pray, the whole building fills up, and on Fridays, the lounge at the front, part of the home of the Imam's brother and his wife, who look after the building (the family has been in control of the building for generations), is emptied of its furniture to make more room to pray. In that sense the building is being used as it always has been. I think that's so lovely. The sense of continuity is complete,' Shabodien says.

OPPOSITE: A little two-storey, 18th-century building in Long Street, originally a house, survives in use as a mosque – for which it was first used early in the 19th century. Originally two palms grew in a garden in front of it – only one of which survives.

PALM TREE MOSQUE
LONG STREET
P
60 min
PARKING
ICE
CLOTHING

RIGHT: On entering from Long Street, the congregation must descend a few steps now that the pavement outside is higher than it once was. The door has been shortened, and the two sash windows facing onto the street are also lower than they would originally have been.

UP FOR AUCTION
FEMALES
ONLY

محمد
الله
salton

ABOVE: The mens' apparel: thobes hanging on hooks with accompanying fezs. This timeless scene could exist anywhere in the Muslim world.
OPPOSITE: The mihrab, on the left, is a niche in the wall that indicates the direction of the Kaaba in Mecca and hence the direction that Muslims should face when praying. In the middle, the minbar, or pulpit, is raised above the floor of the mosque.
PAGES 80–81: Inside, the simple workaday interior is still very much in use by the faithful, many of whose families have been praying here for generations.

OLD MUTUAL BUILDING
Darling Street

An editorial in *The South African Architect* in January 1940 said: 'The Old Mutual has given to the Mother City an architectural landmark of which citizens may be justly proud.' It was right at the time, and it's a pity now that not many get to see what survives within. After all, this building epitomises the Art Deco style. It was designed by Louw & Louw, working with Fred Glennie who, continued the editorial, 'may be congratulated upon the successful planning and completion of a building which pleases the eye and admirably serves its purpose'. It's a building 'which marks at once a new departure and a higher level of achievement in the field of commercial architecture'.

Opened in 1940 as the headquarters of the South African Mutual Life Assurance Society, it is odd that, less than 20 years later, it no longer suited the purpose for which it was intended. Today, most of the space has been converted into apartments, but its labyrinthine corridors and twisting staircases lead to some extraordinary rooms over which the Old Mutual still retains ownership.

These have hardly, if at all, been changed and remain largely as they were executed, a wonderful example of architect, artist and craftsman working in unison to a single vision. Original light fittings survive, parquet floors are still there, and even the original door handles, in many instances, are still in use. There's the tall, narrow gold-veined black marble entrance lobby with its burnished gold ceiling and stainless-steel trim. There's the magnificent colonnaded Banking Hall, where eight columns in red Porto Santa marble extend up through three floors, all its fittings intact, trim and perfectly formed. The frescoed Assembly Room is a *tour de force*: here, in a series of dado-to-ceiling frescoes, artist Le Roux Smith Le Roux depicted the modern history of South Africa – albeit very much a period view – having earned his laurels painting murals for Herbert Baker inside South Africa House in London. And then there are the directors' rooms nearby which, fitted out in South African woods, include a boardroom where, at dado level, there's a continuous stinkwood frieze carved by Ivan Mitford-Barberton with, above it, Joyce Ord-Brown's mural showing Cape Town as the Tavern of the Seas. Here the furniture is intact in its style, representing a transition between the old world and a glorious new one.

What an incredible building; what an extraordinary interior. Hidden from view, this is one of the secrets of the city that should be revealed more frequently to more viewers.

OPPOSITE: The entrance lobby. Black, gold-veined onyx for the walls and burnished gold leaf for the ceiling. At the summit of the 17 steps is the entrance to the Banking Hall, surmounted by a window into which is etched the ziggurat shape of the building.

RIGHT: The Banking Hall is characterized by the slickness of its finishes: the black, gold-veined onyx continues up from the lobby; and here, too, are the characteristic stainless-steel trim and light fittings found elsewhere in the building.

PAGES 86–87: Double-height marble-clad colonnades line the Banking Hall. Between the columns are the coats-of-arms of each of the provinces and countries of Southern Africa in which the South African Mutual Life Assurance Society was present.

PAGE 88: Although much of the building has been converted into apartments, the Old Mutual retains ownership of the significant public areas, of which the Banking Hall is one.

PAGE 89: Hewn from Paarl Mountain granite, this baboon is part of the external cladding of the building. Along with an elephant and a tribal head, it projects from the upper façade of the Darling Street elevation.

SPES BONA

PAGES 90–91: The Assembly Room, one of the finest interiors in Cape Town, is adorned with frescoes done in 1942 by Le Roux Smith Le Roux, depicting the Great Trek, the discovery of gold and, on the right, progress manifest in new railroads and productive farms.
ABOVE: A detail of the panel depicting engineering, the building industry and railroad construction. Is it the English 1930s painter, Stanley Spencer, who springs to mind as the archetype? Or Masaccio or, even earlier, Giotto, both of whose lumpy figures stoically get on with the job at hand – just as Le Roux Smith Le Roux's do here?
OPPOSITE: In this depiction, the Old Mutual Building is heroically, iconically, the focus of modern Cape Town.

LEFT: The Director's Boardroom: at dado level is a stinkwood frieze carved by Ivan Mitford-Barberton. Above it, Joyce Ord-Brown's mural depicts Cape Town as the Tavern of the Seas.

TAJ HOTEL CAPE TOWN

St George's and Wale streets

There can't be many sites in the centre of Cape Town that are more historic than this one. Opposite St George's Cathedral, a stone's throw from the Company's Gardens, at the junction of St George's and Wale streets, round the corner from the Groote Kerk and the Old Slave Lodge, this building has seen it all. Today, with its neighbour on the corner of Adderley Street, formerly the Temple Chambers, it houses the Taj Hotel Cape Town.

It was designed by James Morris (1878–1964) and completed in 1932, beginning life as the original South African Reserve Bank. It's in the context of that role that you must read its design and iconography. Morris had once worked as draughtsman at the firm of Herbert Baker & Massey and, with them, had worked on St George's Cathedral across the road. Later, he was a partner with Baker and FK Kendall in Baker, Kendall & Morris. Under his own steam, however, he designed the Reserve Bank and, for his work, was awarded the Bronze Medal by the Cape Provincial Institute of Architects (1932). This is the man with a number of other interesting buildings on his résumé – including Lourensford in Somerset West (1928).

The external façades have a look of Italian Renaissance architecture about them, in particular the Palazzo Pitti in Florence, a 15th-century palace whose façades, like those of the Palazzo Strozzi, also in Florence, display heavily rusticated, macho stonework at lower levels as a symbol of temporal power, their brute force giving way to finer execution higher up, closer to heaven. In much the same way, the rusticated, no-nonsense Paarl granite of the exterior of the Reserve Bank building was intended to symbolize rocklike financial stability. The associated bronze window grilles and gates enforce the theme.

The most significant portion of the interior is the old banking hall, now the hotel lobby. Planned in the shape of a Greek cross, it has a barrel vault supported by four fluted columns of Portuguese Styros marble. Reg de Smidt, Morris's chief assistant on the Reserve Bank, writes that meticulous planning was taken to ensure the banking hall was bathed in sunlight. 'For every month of 1929, James Morris bludgeoned the Astronomer Royal into measuring the position of the shadows on the skylight. The angle of the sun would create variations of light intensity in the central banking area and Morris wanted direct sunlight in the banking hall.' The hotel has retained this room, which is now used as a lounge and reception area; it's surprisingly small, and rather delicately formed.

OPPOSITE: The entrance to the former South African Reserve Bank is meticulously preserved and in use today as the hotel's front door.
PAGE 98: Lions, sculpted by Ivan Mitford-Barberton, on the bronze grilles on the front façade.
PAGE 99: The handsome former banking hall, now the hotel lobby, has preserved in it the original cream and brown Portuguese Styros marble columns.

SOUTH AFRICAN RESERVE BANK
SUIDAFRIKAANSE RESERWEBANK

CENTRE FOR THE BOOK
Queen Victoria Street

The august Centre for the Book, a veteran of Queen Victoria Street, made its movie debut in 2006. There's a scene in the last few moments of *Blood Diamond*, which stars Leonardo di Caprio and Jennifer Connelly, in which Djimon Hounsou, who plays Solomon, is seen preparing to tell everything he knows about the illicit trade in, and his experiences of, blood diamonds. The setting is a conference in a handsome stone building, pretending to be in Kimberley. In fact, the setting is the Centre for the Book and perhaps, in all its history, it hasn't seemed more alive – particularly when Solomon's entrance to the auditorium is met with a standing ovation as the film ends.

An exceptional Edwardian building, its copper-coated dome topped by a cupola in teak, the Centre for the Book has had a gloomy life, one that began in 1906, when it was officially opened by Sir Walter Hely-Hutchinson as the senate house for the University of the Cape of Good Hope (the forerunner of the University of South Africa). The senate spent most of its early life as an examining agency for Oxford and Cambridge universities – the University was the incubator from which most other South African universities are descended. Designed by Hawke & McKinlay, the problem was that 'the new building lacked quickening academic life to stir its gloomy depths, and through its hollow corridors echoed the footfalls of solitary script-laden examiners, symbolic of its academic emptiness'. A white elephant in other words. It was built before there was a 'real' university, which, said *The Cape Times* in May 1910, was 'like building a town hall where there is neither town nor resident citizens'. It offered examinations but not tuition, and it had the power to confer degrees on successful examination candidates. Olive Schreiner was honoured here in 1913.

Times have changed. While a chunk of the 20th century saw the building being used as the Cape Archives – during which time it fell into disrepair – since the late 1990s, it has come into its own and is now buzzing with activity. 'The Centre for the Book,' says Mandla Matyumza, its executive head, 'is unique in South Africa. It operates under the ambit of the National Library of South Africa, but it is not a library. It's a specialist outreach unit of the National Library and it was modelled on one attached to the Library of Congress in Washington, DC – also a Centre for the Book. It's there to be a catalyst in the promotion of a culture of reading, creative writing and publishing in all local languages and in the provision of easy and free access to books for all South Africans.' The idea was conceived just after 1994, when the State Library and the South African Library amalgamated to form the National Library of South Africa. 'We want to be known for our support in all matters pertaining to books. It isn't easy: how do you encourage people to love books and to read for fun in a country where books are so expensive and people would prefer to buy a loaf of bread than buy a book? So we publish books and donate them to schools and libraries at the heartland of our market throughout the country. That's where our future lies.'

The Centre for the Book has come back to life. It's been restored and it's open for business.

OPPOSITE: The soft sandstone of the upper reaches of the building was the perfect material to support fairly elaborate and often intricate carved decoration. This loggia is above the main entrance, and the exuberance of its detail owes something, however remote, to the decorated sandstone buildings of Lecce in southern Italy.

SPES IN ARDUIS
ANNO

RIGHT: The Ceremonial Hall is nothing like as lavishly decorated as the original plans show. There were spaces for murals on the walls of the drum and the ceilings, but a lack of funds prevented them ever coming to life. The upper book stacks house collections belonging to the National Library of South Africa, including the Louis Leipoldt Collection, while the lower shelves showcase material published by contemporary South African publishers. *PAGE 104:* This bronze and marble bas-relief portrait inside the entrance commemorates shipping magnate and owner of the Union-Castle shipping line, Sir Donald Currie (1825–1909), 'in whose memory £25 000 was given towards the erection of this building by his daughters'. Opposite, a matching bronze commemorates Willem Hiddingh who, similarly, donated £25 000. Both portraits are by W. Reynolds-Stephens (1912). *PAGE 105:* The curved East Corridor, more of an ambulatory, is paved with marble and slate and adorned with pink sandstone columns that later users of the building simply painted over.

SIR·DONALD CURRIE G.C.M.
SPES IN ARDUIS
1825
1909

ABOVE: The building's main feature is the magnificent Ceremonial Hall, designed in the style of a Greek theatre. The flat wall at the back was to have housed an organ, though this never materialized due to lack of funds. Here the graduation ceremonies once took place. *OPPOSITE:* While the base of the exterior is built of Paarl granite, the upper walls are of soft sandstone ashlar that came from what was then the Orange River Colony. Green faïence Spanish tiles cover the roof and the dome is coated with copper and topped by a cupola of teak.

KOOPMANS-DE WET HOUSE
Strand Street

The fact that this house survives at all is something to celebrate. Once at the seafront, Sea Street, now Strand Street ,was lined with dwellings of considerable architectural merit and this was one of them.

Neoclassicism emerged in the Cape in the 1780s, probably following the lead of French-born architect Louis Michel Thibault. Some of the finest townhouses of the period were built at this time; Koopmans-de Wet is one of the very few to have survived comparatively unaltered. Maybe Thibault's work, maybe not, the façade is perfectly classical: four fluted pilasters support a heavy cornice, the inner two a pediment, and beautiful fenestration is symmetrical about a pilastered door case mounted on a raised stoep made out of pretty little Dutch klinker bricks and Robben Island slate.

Marie Koopmans-de Wet inherited the house from her father, whose family had owned it since 1806. She was a society hostess, and many of the leading political and cultural figures of the day were entertained here. But she's remembered for having worked untiringly for the preservation of South African antiques and historic buildings long before any conservation body was established. She helped save the derelict Castle from partial demolition to make way for the new railway, and was instrumental in preserving Groot Constantia. By 1905, for many white Capetonians, English and Afrikaans, a South African identity was interwoven with a pride in a neglected Cape heritage, the rediscovery of which resulted in the preservation of some of its oldest structures. This is the context to Koopmans-de Wet House's own survival. A few years after Mrs Koopmans-de Wet's death in 1906, the house and its contents became a museum.

Where else in the old city can you examine the interior of an 18th-century mansion retaining not only its original layout and decoration, but replete with an assortment of furnishings, porcelain, textiles and paintings that you might have found in the 1770s in Cape Town, 'that great inn, on the highway to the east,' said Charles Darwin. The nucleus of its collection was bequeathed by Mrs Koopmans-de Wet.

But, perhaps most poignantly in the context of modern South Africa, the origins of the divisions between white and non-white are nowhere clearer than at Koopmans-de Wet House. The psychology of division began in houses like this: the white burghers with their dark-skinned slaves; the superiority of the one, the enforced subservience of the other; the illicit liaisons and the half-breed offspring. People aren't really aware of how everybody was put together all those years ago, and we live with the results now. And when those slaves were emancipated, the stereotypes didn't just vanish. Places like this built this nation. Life inside Koopmans-de Wet House was a microcosm of the world outside. And it's all the more poignant here because, while conscious efforts have been made to preserve the domestic context of prosperous 18th-century gentry, unwittingly the life of the slaves with whom they co-existed has been preserved too – although you need a far richer imagination to bring that to life.

Amongst the more tangible legacies is a vernacular urban building style that was adapted to prevent arson by rebelling slaves: the removal of thatch from roofs and wooden shutters from façades; the integration of exterior lighting with door cases to lighten the streets at night; and water channels in front of many of the homes to provide water in case of fire. And in the kitchen, what language were the slaves using, and what were they cooking? Here the so-called 'kitchen Dutch', evolving on ships amongst seafarers of Dutch, Portuguese and Indonesian origin, emerged, a sort of lingua franca amongst domestic slaves known as 'Afrikaaps' – eventually to become Afrikaans. And the food from kitchens such as this is at the core of what would one day give South African cuisine its peculiar character and originality. Here, at houses like this, it all began.

PAGE 108: In the *gaanderij*, or lower hall, the neoclassical wall decoration behind the Cape coromandel side table (*c.*1780) is original – first uncovered around 1913 by Dr William Purcell, whose aim was to restore the house to its original 18th-century appearance.

RIGHT: The dining room, a formal room at the front of the house, is furnished with a mixture of pieces. The dining table is English Regency (1810–1820), while the display cupboard containing Cape and Dutch silver is Cape (1775–1800). On the table is part of a late 18th-century Chinese dinner service. The windows look onto Strand Street.

行藏安於所遇

PAGE 112: Chinese export art painted in the so-called Jesuit tradition (*c*.1820). Two paintings hang in the dining room, and two in the drawing room opposite.
PAGE 113: The windows in the *gaanderij*, or lower hall. From here, the mistress of the house could keep an eye on her slaves' activities in the kitchen courtyard.
LEFT: From her vantage point in the *gaanderij*, with its view onto the front door, the stair and the kitchen, as well as the doors to all the other rooms, the mistress was able to supervise the household activities and see who was coming and going. Both the gate-leg table, made of Burmese teak and stinkwood (*c*.1750), and the Queen Anne-style stinkwood settee (*c*.1770) are Cape.

ABOVE: A collection of landscape paintings hangs in the morning room. Thought to be Italian, they date from the late 18th century. *OPPOSITE:* A detail of the *trompe l'œil* fire surround in the music room. The faux marble is bordered by 'wooden' mouldings and adorned with 'applied' gesso detail. The wall decorations in this house are an exceptional survival.

ST GEORGE'S CATHEDRAL
Wale Street

Once, Cape Town was a distant outpost of the See of the Anglican Bishop of Calcutta. Without a church of its own, the congregation of the time used the Castle of Good Hope for their worship, or they borrowed the Groote Kerk.

But, on St George's Day in 1830, a foundation stone was finally laid for a new church, its design based on London's Greek Revival St Pancras. It would have a classical spire and a portico of Ionic columns topped by a hexagonal steeple freely derived, like that of St Pancras, from the Tower of the Winds in Athens. 'It made one of Cape Town's finest landmarks until it was demolished in 1954,' says Hans Fransen in *A Guide to The Old Buildings of Cape Town*. Inside, it was a simple rectangular box with a gallery, a central altar and a side pulpit.

In 1847, Robert Gray was installed as bishop of the newly created Diocese of Cape Town and old St George's became its cathedral, even though it was too small. Gray was unimpressed with its preaching box characteristics, and its design reminded him of a pagan temple at a time when Christian cathedrals were thought more suitably designed, said Pugin, in the Gothic style. A foundation stone for a new and enlarged cathedral was duly laid in 1901 by the Duke of Cornwall, and the foundations began in 1904. The architects were Herbert Baker and Francis Massey. Baker had by then already built a number of churches in Cape Town. His influence was far-reaching: he stressed simple forms and insisted on the use of 'honest' traditional materials like stone and wood rather than iron and plaster, and leaned towards Early English Gothic as an appropriate stylistic model.

The original plan had a nave with side aisles, a crossing, short transepts, a chancel flanked by chapels, and a rounded east end. The new building was set out along Wale Street at right angles to the old building, the tower of which had terminated the view up St George's Street. The main entrance is through the north transept, which is unusual in a cathedral. The architect, aware both of the hot climate and the difficulty of obtaining good local stone, chose to light the building with small pointed windows. The stone is mostly Table Mountain quartzite, while the roof is covered with red clay tiles. Work was slow, and only in 1936 did St George's begin to look anything like its architects had intended. In the interim, the Duke of Cornwall had became George V, and the South African War, as well as World War I, had been and gone. Today it still isn't finished; it's missing the Gothic tower planned by Baker, which you would have seen as you approached up St George's Street. The cathedral is now the seat of the archbishop of Cape Town.

In 1989, St George's found its true place in history. At the time, it was the seat of Archbishop Desmond Tutu and, because of him, it has become a symbol of democracy in South Africa. It's even been called the 'people's cathedral', mainly because of events on September 13th, 1989. At the time, more than 30,000 people drawn from all races and creeds were led in a mass protest march from St George's by, among others, the legendary Tutu. South Africans would no longer tolerate apartheid. Change was coming. It's thought that Tutu coined an important phrase at the time: 'And so we came to the cathedral to pray: Muslim, Jew, Christian, black, white – our rainbow nation – and as we walked out into the streets of Cape Town it was exhilarating to be joined by thousands, swept along in the realization of the dream that freedom is possible.'

OPPOSITE: The high nave, looking east to the apse. The interior of Baker's cathedral is much more beautiful than its exterior. Inside, it is strong and determined, unlike the outside, which seems unsure of what it wants to be. The archbishop's throne, distant right, is made of wood from the choir screen in Westminster Abbey and given by Lord Nelson.

1936 1952
GEORGII
SEXTI
REGIS

OPPOSITE: The rose window, erected in 1957 in the south transept, is by Frank Spears. The clerestory windows below are by Gabriel Loire (1971). *RIGHT:* Every viewpoint conjures up a substantial Gothic perspective. The stonework, the floor tiles and the wrought-iron work are authentic embodiments of prototypes found all over the English shires.

LEFT: The stalls are made of stinkwood. In front sat the boys, behind them the men and further back the clergy. At the back, adorning the screen, are the arms of the dioceses of South Africa. *PAGE 124:* In St John's Chapel, a monument to Alfred Milner, 1st Viscount Milner (1854–1925), British colonial secretary and architect of the Union of South Africa. It's one of many notable memorials inside the cathedral. *PAGE 125:* Work began at the east end, at the apse, but it was only on completion of the north transept, in 1936, that Herbert Baker's design began to come to life. Baker favoured tall narrow windows in an effort to exclude the brightness of the sun.

N Z
ALFRED VISCOUNT
MILNER
A SERVANT OF THE STATE
GOVERNOR OF CAPE
1897 - COLONY - 1901
TRANSVAAL & ORANGE
1901-RIVER COLONY-1905
HIGH COMMISSIONER
1897-SOUTH AFRICA-1905
BORN 1854 — DIED 1925

WELGELEGEN
Rosebank

Welgelegen is one of the loveliest houses in Cape Town, from the outside. A romantic, asymmetrical cluster of gables and windows, columns and staircases, it was built amongst the trees in the grounds of Groote Schuur by Herbert Baker in 1899. In the foothills of Devil's Peak, its location is spectacular: 'Nature's handiwork is on a larger scale ... in South Africa which the Arch-Architect has designed so essentially in the grand manner,' Baker said in *The Architectural Needs of South Africa*. 'Here the landscape is ... so vast and grand in its general features that the design and disposition of buildings must be conceived on a monumental scale to be in harmony with the work of nature.' While not exactly monumental, Welgelegen, on its slope between the M3 freeway and Main Road in Mowbray, still displays the *genius loci* Baker intended.

The house is one of the most characteristic of Baker's Cape Revival-style dwellings. Cecil Rhodes bought it for his old friend, John Blades Currey, because he'd been so good to him in his Kimberley days, and it subsequently became part of the Groote Schuur Estate. Currey, the man who chose the name Kimberley for the nascent diamond-fields town, was appointed in 1884 as manager of a Kimberley land-owning company and when, some fifteen years later, the company was absorbed by De Beers Consolidated Mines, Rhodes, as chairman of De Beers, invited Currey to become steward of his Cape Town estate. Welgelegen was given to him to live in.

Its interiors showed Baker at his Arts and Crafts best. They survived until 1979, when the university took over the property following the death of its last occupant, Winifred, John Blades Currey's daughter, at 100 years of age. Now, unfortunately, they no longer exist. If you want to know what the home would have looked like, you'd probably have to visit Westminster in the Free State, which Baker designed early in the 20th century for the Duke of Westminster. It's one of the last of his homesteads to survive intact – much of the furniture was designed by Baker himself – and furnished just as he intended. Or you could pop into Welgelegen itself and ask to see the three paintings by English painter, James Durden (1878–1964), which survive there: *The Dining Room* and *The Open Door* being the most interesting. Exhibited at the Royal Academy in London in 1934, these are a record of their time and they're worth examining – if only to establish in your mind's eye what should never have been allowed to happen.

OPPOSITE: The hall, or *voorkamer*, of Welgelegen before World War I was one of Herbert Baker's colonial Arts and Crafts interiors at their best. Scandalously, the house's contents were dispersed on the death of Miss Currey in 1979. Here, the *voorkamer* has been recorded in a painting by James Durden.

ABOVE: Housed at Welgelegen are three paintings by James Durden that depict the house as it was: top, *Exterior of Welgelegen* from the garden; and above, *The Dining Room*, filled with recognizably Cape and English furniture, and a dining table of Baker's own design. *RIGHT:* Terrifically well positioned, the Herbert Baker-designed Welgelegen is a romantically asymmetrical clutter of chimneys, gables and windows – neither Cape Dutch manor nor English country house.

OLD TOWN HOUSE
Greenmarket Square

A plaque at the Old Town House states: 'This building was erected in 1755 as a Burger Watch House, and was used in succession by the Burger Senate and Municipality of Cape Town until 1905. It was given by the city of Cape Town to the Union Government by whom it was restored under the direction of JM Solomon Architect, to house the Michaelis Collection.' And there you have it in a nutshell: a synopsis of the fortunes of an old and venerable Cape Town structure.

Although you might not see it now, there was a time when Greenmarket Square was dominated by South Africa's oldest civic structure. Its baroque façade, attributed to Matthias Lotter, has hardly changed since it was built, but the interior was, over the years, chopped up into a series of rabbit hutches for civic use, particularly in the days prior to the construction of the 'new' City Hall on the Grand Parade. Joseph Michael Solomon, a brilliant young architect from Herbert Baker's firm, was appointed to refurbish the Old Town House to house the fabulous collection of 17th-century Old Master Dutch and Flemish paintings that Lady Phillips, who played a leading role in projects aimed at cultivating and preserving the local artistic heritage, had persuaded Sir Max Michaelis to donate to the Union of South Africa in 1914.

The Cape Times in September 1916 described how 'under the fostering care of Mr. Solomon the barnlike shell, cumbered with mean rooms and stairways, disfigured with boarded ceilings, and littered with unsightly partitions, was transformed into an architectural gem.' Not much of the original 18th-century interior had survived and Solomon, in bringing it back to life, didn't strive to reproduce a period interior either. This is a personal fantasy, albeit one which is the result of considerable research in the galleries and vestibules of genuine 17th-century Dutch guildhalls. In some ways, it is thought that this conversion into an art museum paralleled that of the Mauritshuis in The Hague and, in a way, the Old Town House with the Michaelis Collection can be considered Cape Town's equivalent of the Mauritshuis. In his *Catalogue of the Michaelis Collection,* Professor D Bax praises Solomon as an artist: 'Out of heterogeneous elements he created a harmonious whole in admirable taste, and with such skill that it actually seems pervaded by the spirit of the past.'

The new gallery was opened in 1916 and today it features paintings by Dutch masters including Frans Hals, Jacob van Ruisdael and Jacob Adriaensz Backer. This gift was interpreted as a nation-building gesture in South Africa at that time. Paintings by artists representative of the Golden Age of Dutch culture, given by a British donor, seemed appropriate given that South Africa had then recently become a single new nation with the passing of the Act of Union in 1910. This Act fused the former British colonies of the Cape and Natal with the Transvaal Republic and the Orange Free State into a single entity. A collection of works by the artistic forebears of the Afrikaners, assembled with British money and showing a distinctively English taste in Dutch art, was deemed highly symbolic of political reconciliation and cultural unity at the time, a mere decade or so after the end of the Anglo-Boer War.

The Michaelis Collection remains an open collection and works have been added to it over the decades since it was established. Lady Michaelis gave many additional works after Sir Max Michaelis's death in 1932. The collection has also been expanded by the addition of works on paper, notably etchings by Rembrandt and many other artists. The last acquisition of a major painting was in 1982. With the formation of Iziko Museums, many of the Dutch and Flemish works in the collection of the South African National Gallery are often showcased here.

PAGE 131: Portrait of a Woman by Frans Hals (*c*.1582/83–1666). This significant portrait, albeit of a person whose identity is unknown, is the highlight of the Michaelis Collection. It introduces a note of realism to the portraiture on view here. Her ruddy face and simple outfit – with not a shred of flattery between them – are hallmarks of the painter's later style. *RIGHT:* The architect JM Solomon modelled the staircase on a 17th-century one in the Mauritshuis, a small palace in The Hague in the Netherlands, which was adapted in the 19th century to serve as a museum for paintings. Solomon's domed ceiling is a representation of a southern celestial hemisphere. *PAGE 134: Interior of the Grote Kerk at Bergen-op-Zoom*, by Gerard Houckgeest. One of three church interiors in the collection, it's full of everyday realism. A Roman Catholic church converted for Protestant use, it dates from the years 1443–*c*.1530. *PAGE 135:* In one of the smaller rooms on the first floor, the black and white floor tiles and the terracotta tile-laid fireplace could have come straight from a 17th-century Dutch room, or a Vermeer painting. Was Solomon inspired by something he saw on his travels?

G. HOUCKGEEST
1600-1653.

LEFT: Practically nothing was left of the original interior of the old Burgher Watch House when Solomon set to work on it. For the Frans Hals Gallery, on the first floor, he derived a design from a number of sources in Holland, England and France. The system of bearer and cross-beams in the ceiling, for example, where corbels support the bearer beams, is found in Holland in early 17th-century halls. The parquet floor blocks were sawn from loft beams from the original building. *PAGE 138:* A chunky linen cupboard, from the 17th century, dominates a room on the first floor. Dutch blue-on-white pictorial tiles, which alternate with white tiles in the skirting, depict landscapes. They date from the 18th and early 19th centuries. *PAGE 139:* Solomon took the blue-on-white Dutch tiles of the fireplace in the Print Room from an old house in Kalk Bay. Dating from the 18th century, they depict biblical scenes, giving also book, chapter and verse.

Math 14V22_32
Math: 21. V. 18 24
Math: 26. V. 39.
Johan: 20. V. 16_17.
Math: 27. V. 32.
Math: 28. V. 1_5.
Math: 27. V. 24.
I Sam: 17. V. 40.
Johan: 19. V. 25_28.

ROYAL OBSERVATORY
Observatory

Everything about the Royal Observatory is remarkable. Occupying a piece of land where, uniquely, the original ecology of the area has been preserved, it houses a collection of buildings made famous since its foundation in 1820 through the several important scientific advances that occurred in them. By the turn of the century, the observatory was clearly established as the leader in the southern hemisphere – and easily equal to the best in the northern hemisphere.

In 1832, for example, the distance of a star, Alpha Centauri, was first measured here. In 1842, the first photographs in South Africa were taken by a chief assistant called Charles Piazzi Smyth. The post of Her Majesty's astronomer at the Cape of Good Hope was awarded the Royal Medal on two occasions: the first to Thomas Maclear in 1869 for measurement of an arc of the meridian at the Cape of Good Hope and the second to David Gill in 1903 for researches in solar and stellar parallax, and his energetic direction of the Royal Observatory at the Cape of Good Hope. Between 1885 and 1890 the first sky survey to be undertaken through photography was conducted here. Here, too, Gill's value for the distance between the Earth and the Sun, the fundamental unit of length in astronomy against which all other distances are measured, was determined and was regarded as the best available for 45 years.

The buildings themselves are remarkable. The main building, with its neoclassical entrance, was designed by the British naval architect, John Rennie, and completed in 1828 – the first building in South Africa to be constructed in the Greek Revival style. Today it's missing its original domes. Elsewhere on the property, Herbert Baker's McClean telescope building (1897) survives and features a hydraulically operated rising floor.

The Royal Observatory was founded a few years after the Cape became a British colony, at the instigation of the British astronomical community. It was created by an Order of King George IV in 1820 and was controlled by the Royal Navy. Its purpose was to find accurate star positions and provide a reliable time service to aid the navigation of ships. Today, it is the headquarters of the South African Astronomical Observatory, formed in 1972, and also of the Southern African Large Telescope Foundation, an international partnership. Most of the 19th-century telescopes are still in place and some of them are still used on public open nights to demonstrate astronomical objects. Telescopes that remain more-or-less in operating order include the photoheliograph of 1878, the 6-inch telescope of 1882, the 13-inch Astrographic telescope of 1889, the 24-inch McClean telescope of 1897 and the 18-inch telescope of 1955. In fact, the latter instrument was used well into the 1990s by the late AWJ Cousins to set up precise stellar brightness standards that are still in use worldwide.

Because the city's sky has now become so bright, the best telescopes have been moved to Sutherland.

OPPOSITE: The McClean telescope (1898). The building in which it's housed (*see* overleaf) features a hydraulically operated floor, the intention being that the observer can stand or sit at a convenient height for looking through the telescope. There's a reservoir which stores the hydraulic power at the entrance to the building.

PAGES 142–143: The McClean Observatory Building (1896), designed by Herbert Baker.

NEW SOMERSET HOSPITAL

V&A Waterfront

There is nothing more unglamorous than a hospital. The New Somerset Hospital is no exception. Its appearance, however, is cause for some excitement: a Gothic Revival cake with castellated parapets on the African shores of the Atlantic. It must have been a romantic sight when it opened in 1862. Its style had a purpose: it embodied the governor of the Cape Colony, Sir George Grey's, belief in the moral value of public institutions, for which Gothic was the preferred style in the middle of the 19th century. It was considered virtuous and worthy and Grey wanted it used here.

In 1859, Sir George laid the corner stone at a magnificent ceremony in front of 12 000 people. It was his last public act in the colony and a public holiday was declared in Cape Town. The 'New' hospital replaced the 'Old' one that stood in Chiappini Street on land given by Lord Charles Somerset. Founded in 1818 by Dr Samuel Bailey (who had been surgeon on Nelson's flagship at the Battle of Trafalgar) as a 'Hospital and Lunatic Asylum' for civilian burghers and slaves, the old hospital closed in 1821 and ceased to function.

This new building was the first teaching hospital in South Africa, and was inspired by Florence Nightingale's ideas on hospital design. Its entrance, flanked by massive towers, gave access to a spacious entrance hall, with a long transverse passage on either side, leading to a large stairway lit from above. Additions and extensions to the hospital building were made in the late 19th century and in the early years of the 20th century. The Victoria Wing, which was added to commemorate the Diamond Jubilee of Queen Victoria, was opened in 1897 by Lady Loch, wife of Sir Henry Loch, governor of the Cape Colony. This addition incorporated the Lady Loch, Milner, St Leger and Lightfoot wards. The Lady Loch Ward was kitted out in 1900 with a variety of paintings donated for the purpose.

'Yesterday afternoon,' said *The Cape Times* on November 11, 1900, 'a number of artists who have generously contributed pictures for the beautification of the Lady Loch Ward, visited the hospital in order to view the fruits of their labour. When first the idea of supplying paintings for this excellent object was suggested in artistic circles in Cape Town, the Children's Ward at the hospital was upon the ground floor of the building, but on the completion of the new wing it was decided to remove the little patients to the Lady Loch Ward, and with them the generous works of art that had been given for the beautification of the walls and to delight the hearts of the children.' A hanging committee was appointed to arrange the pictures. 'As it is today,' continued the paper's correspondent, 'the Lady Loch Ward is a perfect art … Many of the subjects selected were from the old nursery books illustrating the better known nursery rhymes while there were also land- and seascapes, pretty little idylls, and in fact pictures representative of every school of painting.'

Who those artists were is a mystery, but their work is still there today – although a recent theft has diminished their number. The nursery rhymes and the tales from the brothers Grimm sit oddly on the edge of the Atlantic in an eerily silent, now unused, children's ward. They're all there, those fantastical people of our past – Little Miss Muffet, Snow White, the Queen of Hearts, the old king in his counting house counting out his money, and the maid in the garden hanging up her clothes, the blackbird poised to strike from the line nearby, a medieval fortress in the distance.

OPPOSITE: This building was designed by Colonial Engineer Scott-Tucker, working with Henry Greaves, from the mid-1800s the architectural director of the Public Works Department of the Cape Colony.

ABOVE: Charming depictions of traditional English nursery rhymes still adorn the walls of the Lady Loch Ward for children, which was opened in 1897.

OPPOSITE: The fortress style of the battlemented, turreted exterior continues within.

PAGE 148: The artists of the works in the children's ward are mostly anonymous. Some were skilled, many weren't, but even in the penumbra of this sad, unused ward their paintings continue to delight.

PAGE 149: From the Lady Loch Ward there are views through the stoep to the Atlantic Ocean.

LODGE DE GOEDE HOOP

Stal Plein

Just to the left of the Tuynhuis, on the edge of the Company's Garden and behind a huge, antique tree, there's a glimpse of it. Mostly out of sight, you'd never know it was there. It's on the other side of the Stal Plein gate, Louis Thibault's extraordinarily simple, whitewashed 'triumphal arch' that hides what was once a garden, in the middle of which stands the old Fountain of Hope. Like the Lodge itself, hidden from view and out of sight, you'd never know it was there unless you'd set out to look for it. Completed in 1803, the Lodge de Goede Hoop, a Masonic temple, is the work of the three greats of early 19th-century building in Cape Town: Louis Thibault, Anton Anreith and Hermann Schutte, respectively architect, sculptor and builder – all of them Freemasons. Unusual, eccentric, odd – these are all words that have been used to describe the Lodge's appearance. In fact, it's a harmonious display of geometric shapes rising upwards and spreading outwards, the severity of its inherent neo-Classicism skewed only by latent Mannerist madness characterized by a stylish ingenuity.

Within, the walls of a handsome octagonal foyer are faced with Coade stone blocks, and there's a niche in each corner. This simple, striking chamber leads to the Robing Room, where two sets of 12-foot double doors, flanked with perfect symmetry by an apse on either side and two pairs of decorative columns, are on axis with the main entrance. Opened, these massive doors reveal the barrel-vaulted Temple Chamber itself, a black-and-white paved rectangle whose dimensions are reputedly based on those of the inner sanctum of King Solomon's Temple in Jerusalem. At the far end of it, on axis with the entrance, is the Master's throne. Placed at intervals along its walls are four late 19th-century statues depicting *Wisdom* (a copy of the Giustiniani *Minerva*, the original of which is in the Vatican), *Strength* (a copy of the Lansdowne *Hercules*), *Beauty* (a copy of the tinted *Venus* by John Gibson) and *Hope* (which was a local creation). These statues were put in place in the late 1890s to replace four by Anreith that, along with much of this chamber, were destroyed by a fire in 1892.

But there's more, and this time it's the real thing. To the left of the foyer is the Preparator's Room with stairs up to the organ loft. Continue going, and you enter the Chamber of Meditation from which, further into the depths of the building, a low, sloping corridor leads to the Middle Chamber. While the Chamber of Meditation is dark, with Anreith's life-size sculpture of Hiram Abiff lying dead in a niche, the Middle Chamber is completely black. Gothic tracery, gilded and marbled, adorns the walls. It's like something out of an early Gothic novel – Horace Walpole's *Castle of Otranto* springs to mind. In a little chapel at the far end is the statue of *Bereavement*, in which a mother laments her dead son, also by Anreith.

On the foyer's right, an anteroom leads to the Chamber of Silence, in which a small table and chair for contemplation are placed in front of Anreith's massive figure of *Silence*, his finger to his lips, an owl on his left arm, revealed if you lift the curtain concealing it.

OPPOSITE: Looking east to the Master's chair, a large part of this chamber, the Temple, was destroyed by fire in the 19th century and rebuilt. Cut into the barrel-vaulted ceiling is the Firmament. Before the fire, four larger-than-life-size statues by sculptor Anton Anreith stood against the flanking walls.

LEFT: The Robing Room is the anteroom separating the entrance foyer and the Temple. Here, members of the Lodge change into their ceremonial regalia.
PAGE 154: Through the portal of the Temple, with its neo-Classical plasterwork, a rigid sightline connects with the front door.
PAGE 155: The Chamber of Meditation, a portion of the Lodge undisturbed by the fire and therefore entirely original, houses Anton Anreith's lime plaster figure of Hiram Abiff, seen through the low passageway that links it with the Middle Chamber.

KNOW THYSELF

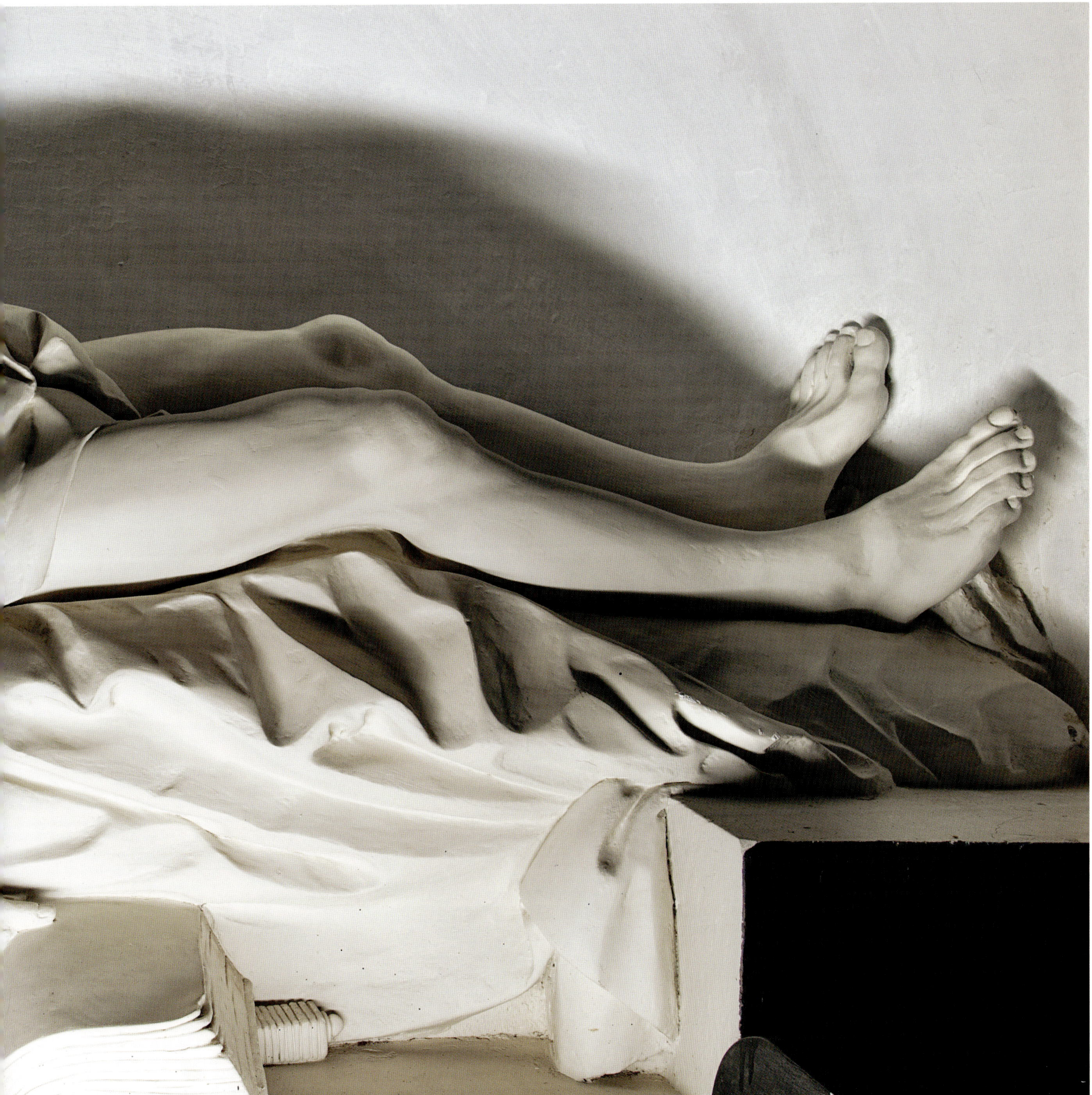

PAGES 156–157: Hiram Abiff in Death, one of the three statues by Anreith to have survived the 1892 fire at the Lodge, and largely unknown to a public well aware of the sculptor's other extant work at the Groote Kerk, the Evangelical Lutheran Church, and elsewhere in Cape Town.

OPPOSITE: The Middle Chamber, viewed from the passageway linking it to the Temple itself.

RIGHT: The Chamber of Silence houses Anreith's *Silence*, his finger to his lips. Filled with symbolism, as are the other sculptures at the Lodge, here the owl on his arm signifies watchfulness.

PAGES 160–161: One of the most extraordinary rooms in Cape Town (1802), the Middle Chamber, with its dark paint and Gothic detail, is entirely original. In the chapel at the east end is Anton Anreith's striking *Bereavement*, in which a widow laments the death of her son.

HUGUENOT HOUSE
Loop Street

Right in the centre of the city, on a corner of Loop and Hout streets, is a remarkable old building that might easily have vanished without trace had a planned ring road been built. Huguenot House, it's called, and it dates from about 1752, the year in which Governor Ryk Tulbagh granted an area of new erven on the northern edge of what was then a small but growing Cape Town.

The house was – and is – fairly handsome; double storeyed and raised on a high stoep, it has five bays, the central one of which projects slightly. It must have been given a makeover sometime in the 19th century, although its original external appearance isn't hard to discern. Although it began as a house, for much of its early life, from 1815 to about 1880, it was a wine merchant's, exporting wine from the Franschhoek Valley.

In 1815 it was sold for a considerable amount of money on the death of its owner, one Nicholas van Wielligh. This represented a spike in its value caused, according to speculation, by the quality and quantity of its interior decoration. During the building's restoration in 1987, neoclassical wall paintings were discovered covering the walls of the rooms on the main floor: the *voorkamer*, the bedrooms to the left and right, and the *agterkamer* beyond. The paintings may date from the late 18th century; the Pompeian reds, and the portraits of the owners and their children as mythological Roman deities, suggest an affinity with frescoes discovered in the Roman city of Pompeii in 1790. On the right wall of the *voorkamer*, Gerharda de Jongh, van Wielligh's wife, is depicted as Luna, and in the *agterkamer*, a daughter is depicted as Ceres and a son as Bacchus. Fanciful speculation yes, but a delicious survival nonetheless. Painted 'mouldings' articulate the walls' surfaces, which are presented as faux-wood panelling.

During restoration, all kinds of other patterned details, both stencilled and marbled, were revealed. They once covered the walls throughout the building. How nice to discover that the old Dutch buildings of the Cape were not simply whitewashed in the way that they are today – and teamed with that uniform green-painted woodwork. One of the bedrooms in Huguenot House had a rose-painted dado, while another had posies of roses, lilacs, daisies and peonies. Elsewhere is a faux painted malachite frieze. Painters from Holland might have spent years decorating the homes of house-proud matrons, sometimes in return for board and lodging. These rooms were opulent, and their tone remains appropriate for the building's current occupants, Prins & Prins Diamonds.

OPPOSITE: When Huguenot house was restored in the 1980s, all kinds of treasures were found hidden from view, including this portrait of a previous prominent owner, Gerharda de Jongh, seen here depicted as the Roman goddess Luna.

Prins & Prins
NS & PRINS
AMONDS
Est.1975
422 1090

LEFT: An 18th-century building at its core, the handsome façade of Huguenot House was both added to and embellished in the 19th century. The high front stoep overlooks Loop Street.

PAGE 166: Painted garlands festoon the fielded panels surrounding the portraits in the *voorkamer* – probably the work of itinerant painters who would have stayed in the house until the completion of the work.

PAGE 167: Enough that's original has survived in this house to enable its history to be pieced together fairly accurately. After construction and until 1815 it was a magnificent private home, and until about 1880 it was the premises of wine merchants. What's here today is the result of a happy restoration carried out for its current owner, Prins & Prins Diamonds.

THE OLD SYNAGOGUE & THE GREAT SYNAGOGUE

Gardens

Enthusiastic attempts at Egyptian Revival styling of prominent façades seems to be a bit of a thing at the southern end of the Gardens. There's the Egyptian Building on the university's Hiddingh Campus over to the west, while in the east, at the top of Government Avenue, there's the Old Synagogue, the *Tikvat Israel* (Hope of Israel) which, although given a front entrance built along the lines of a classical temple, sports some oddly Egyptian Revival-style stucco detail as well.

The Old Synagogue, the oldest in the country, is one of the most beautiful façades on Government Avenue. It is delicate and refined alongside the later, grander and more confident Great Synagogue, an early critic of which thought resembled the Monte Carlo casino. You decide. While today, you enter the South African Jewish Museum via the 'Old' Shul, built in 1863, it's the later one, which dates from 1905, and whose foundation stone was laid by Sir Walter Hely-Hutchinson in 1904, that is regarded as the 'mother' of all South African synagogues.

The story of South African Jewry began in 1806 when Jewish settlers, mainly from England and Germany, began arriving in increasing numbers at the Cape. By 1820, the population had reached about 20, and by 1880 they numbered around 4 000. The character of that original community was predominantly Anglo-German, unsurprisingly, but this was later transformed following significant waves of immigration from Eastern Europe, mainly Lithuania. Many of the newcomers settled in District Six. Towards the end of the 19th century, the Jewish community had been transformed into a significant minority and a new synagogue was needed.

Built alongside the older building, the Great Synagogue, which dates from 1904, is marked by twin towers flanking its Gardens-facing façade, and by a massive semi-circular window above the main entrance. A huge copper-clad dome dominates the interior that holds up to 1 400 people. It's a magnificent building, massive, opulent and majestic, and it cost £26 000 to construct. Today it is part of a campus which comprises the Holocaust Centre, the South African Jewish Museum, the Jacob Gitlin Library, Israel Abrahams Hall, the Samson Centre and, of course, the two synagogues, old and new. At the heart of the old city, it's become the epicentre of Jewish life in Cape Town.

OPPOSITE: In the Old Synagogue, a beaten-metal artwork, *Wings of the Shechinah*, embraces the Ark as part of an exhibition, in 2012, on the life and work of sculptor Herman Wald (1906–1970). In the background, 19th-century stained glass commemorates the death, at 100 years of age, of Sir Moses Montefiore, one of the most famous Jewish philanthropists of the 19th century.

RIGHT: The Holy Ark, containing the Torah scrolls, is housed behind the velvet curtain. Marble, teak, burnished metal and mosaics – some of them gold – enrich the setting. Above is the choir loft.
PAGE 172: The view from the Ladies Gallery of the Ark in a recess of the double-height apse. A copper dome tops this stupendous space.
PAGE 173: The main façade of the Great Synagogue. This is the original main entrance and, facing the Company's Garden across the Paddocks, it dwarfs the more delicate façade of the Old Synagogue on the left.

לא תרצח
לא תנאף
לא תגנב
לא תענה
לא תחמד
כתר תורה
יזכור

אין זה כי אם בית
וזה שער השמים

PAGES 174–175: Teak steps reach up to the *Bimah,* or podium, facing the Ark at the far end. Lateral pews for the men face one another across the Temple, while those in the centre face the Ark. Above is the Ladies Gallery. In the middle distance, the *Ner Tamid* (Eternal Light) sanctuary lamp, a presence in every synagogue, hanging above the Ark, is always burning.

ABOVE: The arrangement of the teak pews in the Ladies Gallery provides the perfect view of the men seated below. Almost up in the 'gods', it is, in fact, pure theatre, as the women spy on their men and young, unmarried females note, for future reference, prospective husbands.

OPPOSITE: The design of this building was, in part, the work of John Parker (1866–1921), and is one of his finest works. The ceilings are an opulent, multi-layered rendition of what early critics thought of as 'casino styling'.

GREEK ORTHODOX CATHEDRAL

Woodstock

There are two St George's cathedrals in Cape Town. This is the 'other' one. While the more famous of the two, the Anglican St George's in Wale Street, is Gothic Revival, this one is neoclassical, which makes perfect sense, given its Hellenic disposition. Built in 1904 for the small local Greek community, its pretty pedimented roof is dominated by a portico, also pedimented, supported by two Ionic columns.

Elevated to cathedral status in 1968, Saint George's, or Agios Georgios, is the seat of the Orthodox Archbishopric of Good Hope, Patriarchate of Alexandria and All Africa, whose mandate includes the Western, Northern and Eastern Cape provinces, the Free State, KwaZulu-Natal, Namibia, Lesotho and Swaziland. It occupies a site in a quiet part of Woodstock and, driving past, there's nothing about the building that says 'look at me.'

Nothing, but nothing, prepares the visitor for what's on view inside: incredibly, the walls, apse and vaults are covered in frescoes. There are protecting saints, some of them feisty on horseback, and there are icons. And, while the Nativity, the Life of the Virgin, and the Agony of Christ come almost to life on the walls of the nave, in the blue-painted vaults – celestial heavens dotted with stars – the Christ Pantocrator stares down at the congregation with that mixture of ferocity and benevolence that marks the facial expressions of Byzantine-style religious iconography. When the sun shines in on these heavenly works through the stained-glass windows, they're bathed in a golden light. Standing here, you could be in a remote monastery somewhere exotically ancient on the edge of the Christian world.

To the untrained eye, at least, the decoration within the Cathedral of Saint George could have been there for millennia. It is most unexpected to discover that a Romanian priest and hagiographer, one Father Nikolai, working in the 1990s with two assistants under the guidance of Bishop Ioakim, who arrived from Greece in 1995 to assist the ailing Archbishop Paul Varnavas, decorated the whole interior. Money to pay for the work, which cost R300 000, was raised by subscription from the members of the congregation. This is not a large building, or even a particularly important one. But its interior is exceptional. There simply isn't anything else like it in the city.

OPPOSITE: The Sanctuary: behind the altar, the crucifix in the apse is dominated by a fresco of the Virgin who, with Christ on her lap, is depicted as Protectress.
PAGES 180–181: From the entrance vestibule, the view down the nave culminates in a screen behind which lies the altar. The religious pictures covering every inch of the walls and ceilings date from the 1990s. The chandeliers and pews were provided by private donations.

ΜΡ
ΘΥ
INBI

ΔΩΡΕΑ
ΑΝΑST ΑΝΑΓΝΩSΤΟΠΟΥΛΟΥ
1940
ΔΕΗΣΗΣ ΟΙΚ. Δ. ΖΗΤΙΑΝΕΛΛΗ 1995
ΔΕΗΣΗΣ ΜΝΗΜΗΝ ΝΙΚΟΛΑΟΥ ΚΑΙ

OPPOSITE: The Archbishop's throne, behind which a frieze of the saints depicts, on the left, St Demetrios and, on the right, St Minas. Beautiful faux drapery provides the dado. *RIGHT:* Heavens above: the ceiling of the nave is adorned with medallions in a celestial landscape. This section is dominated by the Holy Trinity.

BERTRAM HOUSE MUSEUM
Gardens

Bertram House was built in about 1820, at a time when brick houses were fashionable, Britain was in control of the Cape of Good Hope, and a more civilizing attitude to life prevailed. In September 1800, Robert Semple, a Scottish-American merchant who lived briefly in the city, published his impressions of life here, recording that 'the English … are everyday improving and beautifying the town.' Nowhere are the refinements of the day more evident than in this surviving 'house' museum, where the recreated interiors uniquely reflect the style and furnishing fashions of a wealthy English-Cape residence of the Georgian period.

Simple and double storeyed, it is the only late-Georgian redbrick house to have survived in Cape Town. At one time a boarding house, at another an office of the Union Health Department, situated at the Government Avenue edge of UCT's Hiddingh Campus, Bertram House strikes an odd note. One of the many buildings to have been erected in the Company's Gardens, it wasn't always the lone note of domesticity that it is today, partially hidden by a low wall that separates it from the busy traffic of Orange Street, its pretty, weather-beaten façade looking out over a small, tangled garden.

Today, dark and silent inside, it's as dreary as anything until you throw the shutters open and let the sun beam in. What an exquisite little place. The nucleus of its content was provided by Winifred Ann Lidderdale's bequest in 1977. Mrs Lidderdale, whose grandmother had inherited the Mount Nelson estate, with its deer park and lovely grounds where Winifred Ann played as a child, had family ties with the Cape that went back to late in the 18th century. Her great-grandfather, whom Lady Anne Barnard had commended in a letter home, had his country estate at San Souci in Newlands and was a prominent member of the economic, political and cultural life of the colony. His daughter, Mrs Lidderdale's grandmother, received painting lessons from Thomas Bowler. Her painting of the Mount Nelson house and garden hangs in the hall at Bertram House. Childless, Mrs Lidderdale wanted to leave her family's heirlooms and her own collections to a museum that she would establish to commemorate the British contribution to life at the Cape. When she died, aged 95, the South African English press paid tribute to her as a conservator of English culture in the community.

So there it is: Bertram House opened as a Georgian house museum in 1984. 'Particular attention has been given to the interior decoration of an English residence at the Cape of Good Hope,' writes Mary van Blommestein in *Ann Lidderdale and Bertram House: A private dream becomes a public reality*. Not only does her bequest form the nucleus of the collection, but the Lidderdale Trust Fund also makes provision for the purchase of appropriate pieces to augment the original holdings. The bequest comprises 10 major collections, of which the largest is porcelain, mainly English, represented by Spode, Rockingham and Worcester tea sets, and a number of Minton, Wedgwood and Derby dinner and dessert services. There's a collection of English period furniture, including Hepplewhite and Sheraton chairs and sofas, and there are oriental carpets in the textile collection. There's also a brassware collection, and Georgian glasses in the dining room. Elsewhere there's English silver. In Cape Town, this museum is unique.

OPPOSITE: In the dining room at the front of the house, by the front door, new wallpaper was matched to Georgian wallpaper for the perfect fit.

LEFT: After the second occupation of the Cape Colony by the British in 1806, local architecture came strongly under English influence. Between 1820 and 1837, it became fashionable to build Georgian-style brick houses in South African towns. Bertram House, block-like, plain and unadorned, is a unique survivor in Cape Town. The entrance is through the porch, which shields the front door from the Cape's southeasterly winds.

PAGES 188–189: The drawing room, divided by large folding doors, is furnished in the style of the late-Georgian period. On the far left is the desk at which Mrs Lidderdale liked to be photographed.

MULLERS OPTOMETRISTS
Longmarket Street

On a corner of Longmarket and Parliament streets, at the heart of the old city, Mullers is hidden away behind the finest surviving Art Deco shop front in Cape Town. Glossy black and silver chrome, it's a flash of old-world glamour in a neighbourhood that could do with more of it. The shop is still owned by the family of Joseph Muller, who opened here in 1890. An immigrant from Germany's Black Forest, this former jeweller and watchmaker was one of South Africa's first opticians. Past customers, or patients as they might have been called, included Sir Alfred Milner (British high commissioner for South Africa and governor of the Cape Colony between 1897 and 1899 when the Anglo-Boer War broke out) and Sir Walter Hely-Hutchinson (the last Governor of the Cape Colony, appointed in 1901). They would have been drawn to a premises that identified J Muller and Sons as optometrists to the Royal Navy Hospital and, most important, being British, as 'Optometrists by Appointment'.

While the original building dates from the late 19th century, the shop front was added in about 1920. Today, the mirrored interior with its period furniture creates a stylish backdrop for the high tech eyewear of the 21st century. It was from Mullers that Ray Ban sunglasses were first shown to Capetonians in the 1950s, beginning a tradition of bowing to contemporary fashion which continues today with top-of-the-range eyewear from brands such as Oliver Peoples, Prada and Paul Smith, amongst others. Yet, even in a fiercely competitive market, Mullers hasn't strayed from its founder's principle of providing 'Eyewear you can trust'.

OPPOSITE: On a corner of Longmarket Street at the city's centre, the gleaming façade of Mullers has retained virtually all of its Art Deco features.

MULLERS
MULLER'S
104

Mullers est 1890
OPTOMETRISTS

LEFT: Anywhere else in the world, the interior of Mullers would be preserved in a museum of architectural history. The display cases, furniture and lighting are all original.

EVANGELICAL LUTHERAN CHURCH
Strand Street

You get a bit of a shock when you enter this church from noisy Strand Street. From the pavement at its entrance to the dark-stained floorboards within, there's very little in it that's not original. It has an air of antiquity about it, fortified by centuries of polish. Within, it's just wood and pale paint, only the vestry is a golden yellow, its walls from floor to dado covered in faux marbling. All the detail is in the remarkable carvings by 18th-century sculptor, Anton Anreith.

In the early days of the colony, the Dutch East India Company only recognized the Dutch Reformed Church. There was no religious freedom and neither Christians of other denominations, nor anybody else, were permitted to conduct services according to their faith. Petitions to the Lords Seventeen by locals who were Lutherans for permission to erect their own church and provide for the services of their own minister came to nothing. In the middle of the 18th century, Ryk Tulbagh, one of the colony's most popular governors, upheld this rule, yet during his regime, Martin Melck, a member of the Lutheran Church and one of its strongest supporters, succeeded in establishing, on the sly, a place for worship from which this church would eventually be constructed.

Melck, who had come to the Cape in 1746, became one of the richest and most influential farmers in the colony. He acquired plots in fashionable Sea (Strand) Street and here, in 1774, he erected a building that he 'knocked up in the taste of a warehouse' – in fact a barrel-vaulted hall – that, in 1776, he transferred to the Lutheran congregation to use for their services. In 1779, the Lutherans finally got the go-ahead to establish their own church, and between 1787 and 1792 the hall was transformed by Anton Anreith, who redesigned the façade and carved the magnificent wooden sculptures inside – in particular the pulpit figures, today one of the treasures of the city. In essence, that original warehouse-like form survives, although now ornamented around the walls with rows of wooden pilasters, tall, mullioned Gothic-arched windows and stinkwood and yellowwood-panelled galleries, one down each side.

The pulpit, the church's masterpiece, is ornamented with delicious baroque carvings: supported by two life-sized figures of Hercules, each one carrying on his back one of the two front corners of the pulpit, his head and neck bent forward in that pose, employed across Europe in many baroque buildings, to support a balcony or a door case. Behind, massive growling mastiffs support the weight of the back of the pulpit, while underneath it, in the dark, is a recumbent lion that looks as if it was intended for some other position. In 1786, funds were provided 'to buy a slave to keep the pulpit clean.'

The King David relief on the organ loft is also Anreith's; it was executed in plaster, while the supporting cherubs are of gilded wood. The vestry door, once gilded, is also thought to be Anreith's, as is the monument to Martin Melck on the wall to the left of the pulpit. Anreith's lectern, the same date as the pulpit, is characterized by its harp shape and a sculpted swan. A swan, the symbol of Lutheranism, also appears on top of the pulpit's canopy.

In 1810, Hermann Schutte did some additional work on the building. The organ was installed, Anreith's façade was changed and the clock tower was added. Since then, not much has happened here.

OPPOSITE: The King David relief, on the organ loft – beneath which you enter the building from Strand Street – is the earliest example of Anton Anreith's work in the church.
PAGES 196–197: The interior is largely intact. This is a view from the pulpit towards the organ loft. The pulpit, the real masterpiece here, incorporates Anreith's highest achievement of sculpture in wood.

Houdt wat gy hebt, opdat
niemand uwe kroon neeme
Openb: III. vs XI

ABOVE: The pulpit box beneath the rococo canopy is adorned with the winged heads of four smiling cherubs, while a fifth is depicted full-length, supporting the lectern on its head. Behind it is the entrance to the vestry.
OPPOSITE: Hercules, his head lowered as he strains to hold up the structure's bulk, is one of a pair of statues on the pulpit's two front corners. These figures signify the power of faith.

PAGE 200: Beyond the mastiff growling at the rear of the pulpit, the vestry door is also the work of Anreith. The detail of the door itself was once gilded.
PAGE 201: The swan, one of the emblems of Luther and Lutheranism, occurs throughout the church, including on its façade, and on that of the Martin Melck House next door, as well as here, surmounting the pulpit.
RIGHT: From the pulpit, the interior seems to retain the simple shape of the warehouse that it once was. In the background are the organ loft and the front door. Down the sides, the panelling of the galleries is made of stinkwood and yellowwood.

SECUNDE'S HOUSE
Castle of Good Hope

The old fortress of Cape Town is full of surprises. The house where the Secunde lived is one of them. At the heart of South Africa's oldest colonial building, it was where the settlement's vice-governor, the second in charge, or *secunde*, lived and it was built at the end of the 17th century. It's on three floors and, while no original furniture survives inside it, there are curated collections throughout, which help to reconstruct its original appearance as much as can be. Original decoration has been restored – the painted floor tiles in the 17th-century room and the faux dadoes and mouldings.

Part of Iziko Museums of South Africa, three main salons recreate the main periods of its occupation: that of a 17th-century VOC official; his 18th-century equivalent; and an early 19th-century British military officer. These are evocations of what the rooms might have looked like during each period. Over time, the interiors were renewed according to prevailing fashions, and depending on what items the occupants owned and brought with them to the Cape. The Dutch-era rooms are, as one might expect, filled with detail – tiles, woodcarvings and painted floors – as well as the polyglot influences of the occupant's ties to Holland and its colonies in the East. Their contents are chunky and solid and well made. They are full of character and rich craftsmanship, and they hold huge appeal, even for today, particularly since individual items from these periods are highly sought-after and hugely collectable.

In contrast, the British interior has the restraint and austerity that characterized a 19th-century military outpost of the British Empire. It has a variety of furnishings masquerading as one thing when, in fact, all the time they're something quite different – like the campaign bed, which becomes a sofa when not being slept on, and a bureau bed that's otherwise a writing desk. Regency stripes line the walls.

OPPOSITE: In the 18th-century Dutch room, an armoire (1760–1779) hides a remarkable secret: open its doors and the Story of Jephthah from the Old Testament's Book of Judges is revealed. Jephthah led the Israelites in battle against Ammon and, as the result of a rash vow, must sacrifice his daughter after defeating the Ammonites. Here his daughter is seen welcoming him home, unaware of the news he is about to impart. This is period folk art of a type that's increasingly rare.

PAGE 206: The 17th-century Dutch room. To the left of the door is a hefty period *kussenkast*, or linen cupboard, made of oak, ebony and palisander, and topped by a Delft garniture set in a combination of lidded and unlidded vases of 18th-century Dutch tin-glazed earthenware. The floor decoration is original, but restored. The 18th-century Dutch room lies beyond.
PAGE 207: To one side of the 17th-century Dutch room, period polychrome tiles made from tin-glazed earthenware dominate the fireplace. The fireplace itself is not original; it's Dutch, 19th century in 'the style of the 17th century', and came from an abbey in Zeeland in the Netherlands. On the table is a collection of early 17th-century pewter.
LEFT: The oak bed in the 17th-century room originally had doors not curtains. The cradle is Dutch, of the 17th century. The wall painting is from the 18th and 19th centuries.

THE CAPE TOWN RIFLES (DUKES) OFFICERS' MESS
Castle of Good Hope

The establishment of the Cape Town Rifles dates back to November 28th, 1855, in the former Cape Colony. At the time, Great Britain, the colonial power, was faced with a major war with Russia (the Crimean War) and, of necessity, the British Army recalled many thousands of troops from all over the Empire for deployment against the enemy. This included the withdrawal of most of the garrison troops that were stationed here, with the result that, on land, the colony was left largely unprotected. It was against this background that a number of public-spirited Capetonians offered their services to the governor, Sir George Grey, to reinforce the denuded garrison and play an active role in the defence of the colony. Their services were to extend beyond the cessation of hostilities, however, and a permanent regiment, manned entirely by part-time soldiers drawn exclusively from volunteers within the community, was established under the command of Colonel William Hope (1807–1858), a former British Army officer.

In 1867, the regiment's name changed from the Cape Town Rifles to the Duke of Edinburgh's Own Volunteer Rifles, a name adopted in honour of Queen Victoria's second son, HRH Prince Alfred, Duke of Edinburgh, who, at the time, was a captain in the Royal Navy and was on an official visit to the Cape. It was not long before the regiment became popularly known as 'the Dukes'. This is its Officers' Mess, housed in a wing of the Castle of Good Hope.

The Dukes, now the oldest Cape infantry regiment and the second oldest in the South African Army, has been fighting South Africa's wars ever since its foundation. It served in local campaigns, then both on foot and on horseback throughout the Second Anglo-Boer War of 1899–1902, and sent many men to France and East Africa during World War I. When World War II broke out, the Dukes was one of the first infantry battalions to depart for the crucial Abyssinian Campaign, after which it went on to the Western Desert. In the 1970s and 1980s, the regiment was deployed on various counter-insurgency duties in the 'operational area', as well as on several internal security operations, although these deployments ceased when the political situation in South Africa was transformed following the country's democratic elections in 1994. In recent times, the Dukes have become fully committed to the transformation process and now reflect the demographics of the country. But, true to their motto *Semper Eadem* ('Always the Same'), the old standards remain and the regiment's voluntary recruiting and training programmes have prepared it to fulfill the requirements of its current mustering as a sea-landed infantry unit within the conventional forces of the new SA National Defence Force. This includes its present deployments in various parts of Africa, in accordance with the African Union/United Nations peacekeeping initiative.

OPPOSITE: A commemorative plaque presented to Colonel Woodhead, officers and soldiers of the Duke of Edinburgh's Own Volunteer Rifles by General Sir Charles Warren in 1900, during the Anglo-Boer War, in memory of the 'gallant stand' made by the regiment at Faber's Put.

LEFT: The Mess, occupied since the 1930s, is reputedly haunted by a female in 18th-century dress. Thirty-three seats, and the president's chair, flank the table used for formal dinners for serving officers. To the left, on the wall, are the Regimental Colours. In the background, left of the door, is Edward Rowarth's magnificent portrait of Colonel Cecil James Sibbett, the regiment's first honorary colonel (1935–1967), and one-time private secretary to Cecil John Rhodes.

PAGE 214: HRH Prince Alfred, Duke of Edinburgh (1844–1900) for whom the Dukes is named, in the uniform of an Admiral of the Fleet, the Royal Navy's highest rank. The brother of King Edward VII, his nephew became Kaiser Wilhelm II of Germany and his father-in-law was Tsar Alexander II of Russia.

PAGE 215: Down the centre of the table that dominates the Mess is a handsome row of silver shooting trophies and commemorative cups received for heroic acts in battle in various 19th-century campaigns. The city's Jewish community presented the tallest one for Lt Mark Harris, killed during the Bechuanaland Campaign in 1897.

GROOTE SCHUUR
Rondebosch

Herbert Baker's domestic architectural legacy is nowhere more magnificent than here at Groote Schuur, the house he rebuilt for Cecil John Rhodes in 1893, in a style that gave rise to a whole new homegrown architectural idiom.

In the 1890s, the old Cape architectural vernacular, from which Groote Schuur derives its character, was far from popular, but when Baker discovered it, he loved it. 'I carefully studied and made sketches of the architecture of the old houses. When I talked about them to my friends at the Cape, I wondered how little their beauty seemed to be known or appreciated,' he wrote. In recognizing its unique character, he struck a chord with Rhodes, who asked him to work on the restoration of Groote Schuur. Baker went on to borrow elements from the local vernacular, from what he knew of the gabled buildings of Amsterdam, as well as the Flemish connections with his own home territory in England's Kent. And he added his own inventions so that Groote Schuur is, in fact, a fantasy of Edwardian historicism.

When it was finished, it unleashed a flurry of copycat houses marked by double-storey, attenuated gables, barley-stick chimneys, lots of teak and even more whitewash. A whole new architectural style was spawned. Palatial when Cape Dutch buildings were not, of course it isn't really even 'Cape Dutch' at all, but an essay in the romantic Arts and Crafts Movement that preferred vernacular styles to the prevailing industrialism, and which sanctified good craftsmanship and the use of traditional, local materials like stone and wood rather than iron and plaster. This is the building that launched Baker's career as one of the key architects of the British Empire, 'and it was to change the face of South African architecture for ever', says Graham Viney in his book, *Colonial Houses of South Africa*.

The interiors are indebted to the architectural partnership of Ernest George and Harold Peto, where Baker worked as lead assistant between 1882 and 1887. There, emphasis was placed on the importance of working drawings, sketching tours and, above all, respect for high levels of craftsmanship. George and Peto was one of the most successful and fashionable London architectural offices. They were known for picturesque Arts and Crafts houses and their interiors rarely strayed far from a clever set of formulae. You see it all over Groote Schuur: dark panelling contrasting with stone chimneypieces, ornamental brass, white ornamental 'strap work' ceilings and stamped leather or otherwise 'aesthetic' wall coverings. Elsewhere, there are wooden overmantels, or ceilings with small gilt-edged panels between beams that rest on carved corbels. These, along with panelled rooms, floor-to-ceiling chimneypieces in carved stone, tiled inglenooks, and half-landings, are all George and Peto trademarks that were borrowed and used by Baker.

Where once house parties filled the rooms now there's only silence, except for the ticking of the clocks and the occasional door slamming in the distance. Its collections are mostly still *in situ*: Rhodes had agents on the lookout for furniture, books, porcelain, silver and glassware – he particularly wanted items from the Cape. Today the house and its interior remain almost exclusively as they were in Rhodes's day. It's a museum and you can visit it by appointment.

OPPOSITE: The inner hall and landing for the main staircase. Baker designed the chimneypiece in the background. Sitting on the carved teak newel posts is a replica of the mysterious bird sculpture found in the Great Zimbabwe ruins, a stone original of which survives elsewhere in the house. The motif is integrated into the architecture and appears on fire screens, door handles and door fittings.

LEFT: The columned back stoep, above which an open balcony overlooks Devil's Peak and the back of Table Mountain. The heavy furniture is arranged as it would have been in Rhodes's day.
PAGE 220: Everything in this room has the monumentality that Rhodes was after. His taste was for large and impressive pieces, and whatever he or his agents bought had to conform to this ideal.
PAGE 221: The kitchen, an impressive, voluminous space, has the look and appeal of an Arts and Crafts room. The wall cupboard is a typical Baker detail borrowed from the Cape Dutch, although its shape and style is more pronounced than its historic prototype.

RIGHT: In its outward appearance, Groote Schuur is an English country house transplanted to the Cape. Even the bay window on the right has something Tudor about it. But is this house 'Cape Dutch', or is it simply the fantasy of Rhodes and Baker's imaginations?

LEFT: Rhodes's marble-clad bathroom. The massive bath is fashioned out of Paarl granite, while the masseur's table opposite is topped with marble.

HYMNS

CENTRAL METHODIST MISSION
Greenmarket Square

Can this be one of the finest churches in Cape Town? Situated on the corner of Burg Street and Greenmarket Square, the former Metropolitan Methodist Church – now the Central Methodist Mission – was once considered the finest house of worship in the whole colony. Even today, its Gothic Revival interior is much admired.

Before 1876, when the foundation stone was laid, meetings and services were held in a hayloft above a stable in Plein Street and, later, in a disused wine store in Barrack Street. In 1829, a more permanent site was found and the Wesleyan Methodist Church was opened on the corner of Burg and Church streets. Later, inevitably, a larger building was needed and the congregation moved to a new building on the present site.

This Gothic Revival church was designed by Charles Freeman, a versatile architect whose other major adornment of the city was the neo-Classical Standard Bank building on the corner of Darling and Adderley streets – one of his best buildings in fact. His, too, were the original designs for the Houses of Parliament, and he designed that enormous Dutch Reformed Church in the middle of Graaff-Reinet.

During the second part of the 19th century, so pervasive was the idea that Gothic was the only proper style for churches, that many denominations which might normally have favoured a more austere setting eventually capitulated to it. The Methodist church on Greenmarket Square is one of these. Even so, its elaborate finishes and fittings, including an organ, choir, pulpit and communion table grouped together at the chancel end, restate the essentials of the preaching church, distinguishing it from Anglican or Roman Catholic churches of the same style.

Hans Fransen, in his book *A Guide to the Old Buildings of the Cape*, is very enthusiastic about the church. 'It is a basilica type of church, has a short chancel, with the lean-to roof of the aisles broken by a series of gabled transverse roofs. A prominent tower with a tall spire stands on the corner, beside the nave at the head of the aisle. The building has fine dressed-shale walls, its plinth in granite, and an interior of great beauty with its high timbered roof and a gallery supported by cast-iron columns. Its Gothic Revival sculptured stonework is equalled only by that of the Oudtshoorn DRC Church.'

Many prominent Capetonians have been members of the congregation, and the church was famous for the standard of its preaching and for its outstanding choirs. The first radio broadcast of a church service in South Africa was beamed from the Metropolitan Church in 1928 and large crowds gathered outside to hear it. During the 1960s, the church continued to attract large congregations until urban expansion and other factors began to take their toll and the congregation declined. Today, the Central Methodist Mission includes the congregation of the former Buitenkant Street Methodist Church, renowned as a place of sanctuary in the 1980s for detainees and victims of police brutality. (It now houses the District Six Museum.)

OPPOSITE: This church is often regarded as one of Charles Freeman's most significant designs. He is the architect who played a key role in transforming the physical face of Cape Town at the time.

LEFT: The church's high Victorian Gothic Revival interior is completely intact, and unique in Cape Town. On the wall of the right aisle, above the pews, is a memorial to the Revd. Barnabas Shaw (1821–1902), regarded as the founder of South African Methodism.

LEFT: A paean to the memory of the Irwin family, this stained-glass window in the right aisle is one of a handful to have survived. *OPPOSITE:* Cast-iron columns support the Gothic arches of the nave. Freeman was renowned for having taken advantage of new prefabricated techniques and became the local agent for Walter MacFarlane & Co.'s decorative cast iron, which embellishes many Cape Town buildings of the period.

IRMA STERN MUSEUM
Rosebank

The Firs, in Cecil Road, Rosebank – the home where the painter Irma Stern (1894–1966) lived and worked for almost 40 years – houses the biggest collection of her work in South Africa, as well as her collection of rare African artefacts, some of which make frequent appearance in her still-life paintings.

Although Stern was inspired by her journeys into Africa and elsewhere, it's here that she returned to paint, to this richly exuberant home of hers, surrounded by carvings and artefacts, European furniture and sculpture and, outside, a large camellia, palm and strelitzia-filled garden. Her vivid yellow studio is as bold and as vigorous as her paintings, the finest of which demonstrate her grasp of the expressive use of colour.

'I think her epic lifestyle and extraordinary presence have left a distinct stamp on the style of this house, and her personal taste adds to her mystique. But it's an artist's house and it's filled with high-quality objects that she'd collected for their purity and integrity,' says Christopher Peter, the museum's director. 'She responded to them in a visceral way; they inspired her work and are a part of her intellectual creativity. It's not a flamboyant house. It's not an antiquarian's house either, or a feminine one. It's an interested artist's house. It has a sombre quality. It's melancholic. It's the home of a person driven to create as an emotional outlet.'

Her dining room, perhaps the second most important room in the house, is crammed with carved and painted furniture, and with saints and religious icons with myriad provenances, ranging from 15th-century Spain to 19th-century English neo-Tudor. Painted oxblood red, it was the scene of lunches and dinners where Stern, described as resembling an officiating pope, presided over ebullient, colour coordinated settings and heaps of food.

'Each course,' writes Rebecca Hourwich Reyher, who came to lunch in October 1924, 'was served on a tier of dishes and doilies: first there was bouillon; then cauliflower from a head that almost covered a turkey sized platter, and asparagus … After a mountain of vegetables had been consumed, the waitress brought forth a platter of roast beef, a twin platter of roast chicken, a heap of Yorkshire pudding, some peas, potatoes and cabbage, plus a tomato and lettuce and mayonnaise salad. This light repast was topped by chocolate pudding, canned peaches, & whipped cream and a pink and tan candy encrusted macaroon layer cake.'

Controversial in her lifetime, and larger than life, Stern's stylistic innovations disrupted the reserve of a cautious, conservative provincial public. But, by the time she died, her career as a Modernist painter, and her contribution to South African Modernism, marked her as one of South Africa's most important artists. And her popularity as a collectable artist has skyrocketed in recent years. At auction, records for the sale of her works have been broken time and again, with the last recorded (September 2011) price at auction being R21-million for *Two Arabs* still in its original Zanzibar frame. Stern's Zanzibari works are among her most sought-after. 'They represent aspects of the painter at the heights of her creative powers,' said Professor Neville Dubow, a former director of the museum, at the 1982 opening of her exhibition, 'Irma Stern in Zanzibar 1939–1945'.

OPPOSITE: The walls of The Firs are covered in Stern's paintings – some of them among her best works. 'Recently the hype about the extraordinary prices that have been achieved for her work has brought people into the museum,' says director Christopher Peter. 'It's heightened their awareness of it; that kind of money just seems to excite people. It's been quite useful I suppose. That awareness hasn't happened before.'

Irma Stern
1948

OPPOSITE: Vivid yellow, Stern's studio survives, as bold and as vigorous as her paintings, the finest of which demonstrate her grasp of the expressive use of colour.
RIGHT: The death dance is a well-known subject in Western art. A variation on the theme can be seen in the four panels of a cupboard in Stern's studio, which she painted early on in her life.

PAGE 236: Looking from the dining room towards the curator's office.
PAGE 237: Portrait of Dr Louis Herrman, 1922. Herrman was the principal of Cape Town High School and a writer and leading Cape Town intellectual. This painting is a study of a man's character as suggested by his appearance.
LEFT: The dining room is filled with antique furniture, both painted and carved, and with a variety of European religious icons. This was the hub of Stern's home, where she entertained and held court.

CONTACT INFORMATION

Cape Town Rifles (Dukes) Officers' Mess Tel. (021) 597-2902
Central Methodist Mission www.cmm.org.za
Centre for the Book www.nlsa.ac.za
City Hall www.capetown.gov.za
Founder's House, Bishops www.bishops.org.za
Groote Kerk www.grootekerk.org.za
Groote Schuur Tel. 083 414-7961 (tours by appointment)
Huguenot House www.prinsandprins.co.za
Irma Stern Museum www.irmastern.co.za
Iziko Bertram House Museum www.iziko.org.za
Iziko Koopman's-de Wet House www.iziko.org.za
Iziko Old Town House www.iziko.org.za
Iziko Secunde's House www.castleofgoodhope.co.za
Lodge de Goede Hoop www.grandlodge.co.za
Mount Nelson Hotel www.mountnelson.co.za
Muller's Optometrist www.mullers.co.za
Nederlandse Gereformeerde Kerk Tafelberg www.tafelbergkerk.co.za
Old Synagogue & Great Synagogue www.gardensshul.org
Palm Tree Mosque www.muslim.co.za
Royal Observatory www.saao.ac.za
Sendinggestig Museum Tel. (021) 423-6755
South African National Library www.nlsa.ac.za
St George's Cathedral www.stgeorgescathedral.com
Taj Hotel Cape Town www.tajcapetown.co.za
Welgelegen www.uct.ac.za

BIBLIOGRAPHY

D Bax, Litt. D., *Catalogue of The Michaelis Collection*. First revised re-issue. Printed for the Trustees by Rhodes National Heritage Trust, Cape Town, 1981.

Vivien Bickford-Smith, Elizabeth van Heyningen and Nigel Worden, *Cape Town in the 20th Century*. David Philip Publishers, 1999.

David Bloomberg, *The Chain Gang. Mayors who served in Cape Town's City Hall*. Ampersand Press, 2011.

Phillida Brooke Simons, *John Blades Currey 1850–1900*. Brenthurst Press, 1986.

John Dorrington, *Semper Eadem. The Cape Town Rifles (Dukes) 1855–2010*. DEOR Trust, 2010.

Richard Elphick and Rodney Davenport (eds), *Christianity in South Africa: A Political, Social and Cultural History*. University of California Press, 1997.

Dorothea Fairbridge, *Historic Houses of South Africa*. Oxford University Press, 1922.

H Fransen and M Cook, *The Old Houses of the Cape*. AA Balkema, 1955.

Hans Fransen (compiler), *A Guide to the Old Buildings of the Cape*. Jonathan Ball Publishers, 2004.

Hans Fransen (compiler), *Michaelis Collection: The Old Town House, Cape Town. Catalogue of the Collection of Paintings and Drawings*. Wanders Uitgevers, Zwolle, 1997.

John Gardener, *Bishops 150. A History of the Diocesan College, Rondebosch*. Juta, 1997.

D Greig, *Herbert Baker in South Africa*. Purnell and Sons, 1970.

Thelma Gutsche, *The Life & Times of Florence Phillips*. Howard Timmins, 1966.

The Hellenic Community of Cape Town 1900–2000, a history of 100 years. Interamerican with New Media Publishing, 2000.

Michael Keath, *Herbert Baker. Architecture and Idealism 1892–1913. The South African Years*. Ashanti Publishing Ltd, 1992.

JJ Oberholzer, *The Historical Monuments of South Africa*. Rembrandt van Rijn Foundation for Culture, 1972.

Neil Orpen, *The 'Dukes' – A History of the Cape Town Rifles (Dukes)*. Cape Town Rifles Dukes Association, 1984.

David McIntyre, *A Century of Bishops*. Juta & Co Ltd., 1950.

James B Sherwood with Ivan Fallon, *Orient-Express, A Personal Journey*. The Robson Press, 2012.

Malcolm Taylor, *A History of Rugby Football and Cricket at the Diocesan College*. The Diocesan College, Cape Town.

VASSA Journals, Number 10, 2003; 19, 2008.

Graham Viney, *The Colonial Houses of South Africa*. Struik Winchester, 1987.

Graham Viney and Phillida Brooke Simons, *The Cape of Good Hope 1806–1872: Aspects of the life and times of British society in and around Cape Town*. Brenthurst Press, 1994.

Michael Walker, *The Early Architects of Cape Town and their buildings (1820–1926) with postcard illustrations*. The Kalk Bay Historical Association, 2012.

Robert Whyte, *St Andrew's Presbyterian Church, Cape Town. A Centenary Record. 1829–1929*. Presbyterian Bookroom, 1929.

Nigel Worden, Elizabeth van Heyningen and Vivian Bickford-Smith, *Cape Town – the Making of a City*. David Philip Publishers, 1998.